D0948993

MALCOLM X

MALCOLM X

A Biography

A. B. Assensoh and Yvette M. Alex-Assensoh

GREENWOOD BIOGRAPHIES

 GREENWOOD

AN IMPRINT OF ABC-CLIO, LLC
Santa Barbara, California • Denver, Colorado • Oxford, England

Library of Congress Cataloging-in-Publication Data

Assensoh, A.B.
  Malcolm X : a biography / A.B. Assensoh and Yvette M. Alex-Assensoh.
    pages cm. — (Greenwood biographies)
  Includes bibliographical references and index.
  ISBN 978-0-313-37849-2 (hardcopy : alk. paper) — ISBN 978-0-313-37850-8
(ebook)   1. X, Malcolm, 1925–1965.   2. Black Muslims—Biography.
3. African Americans—Biography.   I. Title.
  BP223.Z8L57166   2014
  320.54'6092—dc23
  [B]   2013029454

ISBN: 978-0-313-37849-2
EISBN: 978-0-313-37850-8

18 17 16 15 14   1 2 3 4 5

This book is also available on the World Wide Web as an eBook.
Visit www.abc-clio.com for details.

Greenwood
An Imprint of ABC-CLIO, LLC

ABC-CLIO, LLC
130 Cremona Drive, P.O. Box 1911
Santa Barbara, California 93116-1911

This book is printed on acid-free paper ∞

Manufactured in the United States of America

CONTENTS

SERIES FOREWORD

In response to school and library needs, ABC-CLIO publishes this distinguished series of full-length biographies specifically for student use. Prepared by field experts and professionals, these engaging biographies are tailored for students, who need challenging yet accessible biographies. Ideal for school assignments and student research, the length, format, and subject areas are designed to meet educators' requirements and students' interests.

ABC-CLIO offers an extensive selection of biographies spanning all curriculum-related subject areas, including social studies, the sciences, literature and the arts, history and politics, and popular culture, covering public figures and famous personalities from all time periods and backgrounds, both historic and contemporary, who have made an impact on American and/or world culture. The subjects of these biographies were chosen based on comprehensive feedback from librarians and educators. Consideration was given to both curriculum relevance and inherent interest. Readers will find a wide array of subject choices from fascinating entertainers like Miley Cyrus and Lady Gaga to inspiring leaders like John F. Kennedy and Nelson Mandela, from the greatest athletes of our time like Michael Jordan and Muhammad Ali to the most amazing success stories of our day like J. K. Rowling and Oprah.

While the emphasis is on fact, not glorification, the books are meant to be fun to read. Each volume provides in-depth information about the subject's life from birth through childhood, the teen years, and adulthood. A thorough account relates family background and education, traces personal and professional influences, and explores struggles, accomplishments, and contributions. A timeline highlights the most significant life events against an historical perspective. Bibliographies supplement the reference value of each volume.

INTRODUCTION

On February 21, 1965, Malcolm X entered Manhattan's Audubon Ballroom to address an assembled large crowd, which included his supporters, admirers, and family members, mainly to speak about the newly-formed Organization of Afro-American Unity (OAAU). As he was about to start his speech, a young black man in the audience intentionally tried to cause a commotion by shouting, "Nigger! Get your hand outta my pocket." Characteristically, Malcolm moved forward, with his bodyguards looking on, to stop the commotion that was erupting. It was at that moment that he was shot in the chest once with a double-barreled sawed-off shotgun by a man sitting in the front of the auditorium. Subsequently, two other men charged the stage and fired semiautomatic handguns, striking Malcolm several times. The ballroom was covered with blood, and several bullet holes riddled the walls. In the aftermath of the melee and the shootings, one of the suspected gunmen, by the name of Talmadge Hayer (also known as Thomas Hagan), was seized at the murder scene and severely beaten by the crowd before New York area policemen arrived to rescue him. The other gunmen escaped immediate capture. Malcolm was rushed to New York's Columbia Presbyterian Hospital, where he was pronounced dead at 3:30 P.M. An autopsy report revealed 21 gunshot wounds on several parts of his body.

The viewing of his mortal remains attracted a large crowd of mourning spectators. Thousands of Harlem residents went to Harlem's Unity Funeral Home between February 23 and 26, 1965, for the purpose. However, the actual funeral for Malcolm X was held on February 27 at the Faith Temple Church of God in Christ, also in Harlem, with not less than 1,000 persons from all walks of life in attendance. Also, many African American leaders attended the funeral, and the eulogy was preached by Malcolm X's friend, Ossie Davis. Like other black leaders, Mr. Davis had positive comments to make about Malcolm X to contrast past negative comments made by the critics of him. Among other laudable words he spoke as part of his eulogy, Mr. Davis said to a thunderous applause: "Malcolm was our living, black manhood! This was his meaning to his people. And, in honoring him, we honor the best in ourselves."[1]

Malcolm X, at the time of his death, had transformed his life and become a respectable American citizen. Seasoned scholars and young students in the 21st century have made efforts to seek edification from his sayings and writings, including his autobiography.[2] Nationally, he has since then also been seen in a different positive light; therefore it was not surprising that on January 20, 1999, Malcolm was honored by the U.S. Postal Service, which issued a special commemorative postage stamp. About the stamp, Attallah Shabazz, his oldest daughter, *inter alia,* wrote: "The stamp also serves as a reminder of the stock from which we were born and confirms significantly that how one lives his or her life today stands as a testament to one's [legacy] forever after."[3]

Malcolm X used his Nation of Islam (NOI) membership and, later, leadership to help transform the lives of many young African American men and women. For these young men and women, Malcolm was a teacher, a parent and, above all, a mentor of unlimited magnitude. Malcolm X was therefore seen like a modern-day Marcus Josiah Garvey, the Jamaican nationalist, who migrated to Harlem to lead a nationalist movement, which had "Back to Africa" as its motto and clarion call. Malcolm's positive deeds and his overall posture of taking part in efforts, through the NOI, to transform desperate African

American lives, to make lost young men and women feel loved and with hope, prompted Mr. Davis, in his eulogy, to see him as the African American's ultimate "living black manhood."

In this biography, we have also shown that Malcolm X was not only an important American citizen but also an iconic figure within the context of pan-Africanism—the movement that was used to promote continental and international black consciousness by Dr. W. E. B. Du Bois (United States) as well as such continental African leaders as Presidents Kwame Nkrumah (Ghana), Jomo Kenyatta (Kenya), Julius K. Nyerere (Tanzania), Gamal Abdel Nasser (Egypt), Kenneth Kaunda (Zambia), Milton Obote (Uganda), and Patrice Lumumba, among others.

Malcolm X's travels to the Middle East to perform the Islamic pilgrimage in Mecca and his extensive travels in Africa, during which he was well received by African leaders, marked him as a leader who could stand tall in the annals of African decolonization as well as the civil rights movement, through which his African American compatriots sought to bring about meaningful freedom and justice for all of America's downtrodden, including those that University of Chicago sociology professor William Julius Wilson described as the underclass.

As an African American leader who led such social movements as the Organization of Afro-American Unity (OAUU) and also championed the causes of the NOI, Malcolm X today stands out as one of the unique and selfless African American leaders, whose positive deeds are worthy of mention in such a biography. Like his compatriot, Rev. Dr. Martin Luther King, Jr., Malcolm X eventually paid the ultimate sacrifice with his precious life when, on that fateful February day in 1965 in Manhattan's Audubon Ballroom, his life was cut short by an assassin's bullet.

Ossie Davis was not gainsaying when he also concluded in the Malcolm X eulogy that, indeed, the assassinated African American leader was, above all, African America's shining armor.[4] We, therefore, deem it auspicious to share the life and times of Malcolm X with a wider audience through this biography. The publication is necessary today and also in the future because there are many young African American men and women, who have heard the name of Malcolm X. Yet, they never had the opportunity to read, in detail, about his numerous accomplishments and deeds. This biography may therefore be the only medium through which they will study the life and times of the iconic figure known as Malcom X, a real shining armor as well as the ultimate living black manhood, whose exemplary life is worth reading about and studying.

TIMELINE: EVENTS IN THE LIFE OF MALCOLM X

1919   Earl Little, a Baptist preacher from Georgia, marries Louise Langdon Norton, a native of Grenada in the former British West Indies.

1920   On February 12, the first of the 10 children of Earl and Louise, named Wilfred, is born in Philadelphia, Pennsylvania.

1923   Earl and his wife move with their three children to Omaha, Nebraska, for Earl to start as the representative of Marcus Garvey's Universal Negro Improvement Association (UNIA).

1925   On May 19, Malcolm X is born as Malcolm Little at University Hospital in Omaha, Nebraska.

1926   The family, accompanied by their four children—with Malcolm being the youngest at the time—move to Milwaukee, Wisconsin.

1927   Malcolm X's younger brother Reginald is born in Milwaukee, Wisconsin; shortly after his birth, he is found to have a hernia problem, which is left untreated.

1928   The family moves to Lansing, Michigan, where Earl starts as a Baptist preacher and, for the first time, buys a house for the family.

1929   In November, the Little's Lansing home is burned to the ground.

In December, Earl uses his savings to build another home on the outskirts of East Lansing, Michigan.

1930   Followers of W. D. Fard, a well-known Islamic leader, establish the first Temple of Islam in Detroit, Michigan.

1931   In January, Earl and Louise enroll five-year-old Malcolm in kindergarten at Pleasant Grove Elementary School.

On September 28, Malcolm's father, at age 41, is killed by a streetcar and reports indicate that he might have fallen off the vehicle; however, blacks suspect foul play that might have been orchestrated by a local white supremacist group. An announced official inquest confirms the death as being accidental.

1938   Malcolm completes seventh grade in the West Junior High School in Lansing, Michigan, the same time that his mother, Louise, starts to show signs of mental illness.

1939   It is confirmed that Louise is suffering from a mental illness, and she is committed to a state mental institution in Kalamazoo, Michigan. She remains in the asylum for 26 years.

In May, Malcolm, with seventh-grade education, begins part-time work as a houseman for Dr. Gertrude Sullivan.

In August, a social worker recommends that Malcolm be placed in what was known as a juvenile home since his mother is to remain in the mental health institution for a while.

In the fall, Malcolm is persuaded to return to school, and he begins at Mason High School in Mason, Michigan.

1940   Due to adjustment problems, by the middle of this year, Malcolm has been reassigned to various foster homes; moving from place to place was also a way for social workers to find a proper fit for young Malcolm Little.

1941   In February, Malcolm moves in with his half-sister, Ella, in Boston, Massachusetts, as he had nowhere else to stay.

By the beginning of the summer of this year, Malcolm works in a shoeshine business as well as a part-time dishwasher, soda jerk, and a part-time railroad employee.

By this time, in the fall, Malcolm's sister objects to her half-brother's involvement with several shady and suspected criminal characters during his stay in Boston.

1942   Malcolm Little, at age 17 but too tall for his age, moves to Michigan and works as a porter-messenger.

1943   At 18 years of age, Malcolm Little moves to New York to start work for the New Haven Railroad and also as a part-time waiter, bartender, and dancer at a local restaurant.

In summer, a U.S. Army recruiter who interviews Malcolm Little finds him unfit for military service due to the way he answers questions during his interview.

1944   Malcolm returns to Boston and obtains a job for the local Sears and Roebuck, Company.

In November, Malcolm is indicted and brought to court for larceny and given a three-month suspended sentence. He is placed on probation for one year.

1945   Malcolm moves back to New York, where he starts work as a dancer.

In December, Malcolm and his friends travel to Boston to engage in a series of burglaries.

1946   In January, Malcolm is arrested when he attempts to reclaim a stolen watch that he left for repair at a Boston jewelry store. He is indicted for firearms possession, larceny, a break-in, and forcible entry. Court finds Malcolm guilty.

In February, upon being sentenced by the local court, Malcolm begins serving his 8–10-year sentence at Charlestown, Massachusetts.

1948   While in prison, two of Malcolm's brothers (Wilfred and Reginald) introduce Malcolm to the teachings of the Honorable Elijah Muhammad and his Nation of Islam (NOI).

In March, with the help of Ella, Malcolm is transferred to Norfolk Prison Colony in Massachusetts, which provides him with excellent access to books and other reading material, which therefore starts Malcolm Little's self-education.

1950   Through Islamic teachings and Islamic reading materials, Malcolm becomes a model prisoner. He also tries to recruit other prisoners for the Islamic religion, as he considers himself an informal Muslim.

1952   On August 7, Malcolm is paroled by the Massachusetts state prison system, released from prison, and he travels to Detroit to live with his older brother, Wilfred, and his wife, Ruth. While in Detroit, his brother helps him find work as a furniture salesman.

On August 20, Malcolm seeks and receives permission from his parole officer to accompany a delegation of the Detroit NOI branch, during which he encounters for the first time the NOI leader, the Honorable Elijah Muhammad, who was wearing a gold-embroidered fez. Malcolm publicly receives the blessing of Muhammad and, that summer, confirms the change of his name from Malcolm Little to Malcolm X.

Back in Detroit in September, Malcolm starts work for Cut Rate department store to fulfill his parole condition that he finds a job, instead of remaining idle. His main plan is later on to work for Ford Motor Company.

1953   Malcolm begins work on the assembly line at Ford Motor Company, and also begins to attend NOI meetings.

On May 4, the Massachusetts Parole Board certifies Malcolm X's discharge from parole.

In June, Malcolm travels to Chicago for brief instructions in Islam, where he lives with NOI members. He is later appointed to serve as an NOI assistant minister of Detroit Temple No. 1.

1953   In September, Malcolm becomes the first minister of Boston Temple No. 1.

1954   Malcolm serves as a minister and speaker at various Muslim temples. In June, he becomes the minister of New York Temple No. 7.

1955   For the first time, Malcolm hears rumors that Muhammad is an adulterer, and that he has fathered some children out of wedlock.

1956   Betty Sanders joins New York Temple No. 7 and, as a new Islamic convert, she changes her name to Betty X.

1957   Hinton Johnson, a member of NOI, is beaten by police and jailed. Malcolm gathers a contingent of Muslims from Temple

No. 7 in New York in front of the police station and demands that Johnson be taken to the hospital.

1958   On January 14, Malcolm marries Betty X. After their marriage, Malcolm and his new bride initially decide to live in an apartment in East Elmhurst, Queens.

In November, Malcolm and Betty's first child, Attalah, is born.

1959   Television documentary involving Malcolm, titled "The Hate That Hate Produced," is aired.

In July, Malcolm pays brief visits to United Arab Republic of Egypt, Sudan, Nigeria, Mecca, Iran, Syria, and Ghana as Muhammad's ambassador.

1960   Malcolm debates with William M. James on WMCA radio regarding the topic of "Is Black Supremacy the Answer?"

In December, Malcolm and Betty's second daughter, Qubilah, is born.

1961   Malcolm speaks at Harvard Law School forum and debates Walter Carrington of the NAACP.

On January 18, Malcolm leads a protest of Muslims in front of the United Nations to protest the murder on January 17 of Prime Minister Patrice Lumumba of the Congo (now known as the Democratic Republic of Congo, DRC).

1962   Malcolm engages in several speeches on college campuses and in Chicago, New York, and Los Angeles regarding racial discrimination and oppression and the futility of integration strategies.

1962   In July, Malcolm and Betty's third daughter, Ilyasah, is born.

In early fall, Malcolm X continues to deliver speeches about racial oppression and police violence.

In December, a few days before Christmas and with seasonal gifts in hand, Malcolm X speaks with Muhammad's three former secretaries, all of whom have children for him. Malcolm learns that NOI members are leaving the Chicago mosque because of Muhammad's adultery.

On December 25, Malcolm senses strains between his family and Muhammad's family, hence, no Christmas gifts would be exchanged. Consequently, Muhammad's son (Herbert) reportedly directs the editor of the NOI news-magazine, *Muhammad Speaks*, to minimize Malcolm's coverage in the publication.

1963 In May, *The New York Times* reports Malcolm X's criticism of President Kennedy for his handling of the Birmingham civil rights crises.

In mid-May, *Amsterdam News*, a major black newspaper in Harlem, reports that Malcolm attacks Martin Luther King, Jackie Robinson, and Floyd Patterson mainly because of their work for racial integration that the NOI does not support.

In August, Malcolm continues to speak in various cities around the country, and he attends the march on Washington as a silent observer.

On November 22, President John F. Kennedy is assassinated.

In December, Malcolm gives his now infamous "Chickens Coming Home to Roost" speech.

Three days after giving the December speech, Malcolm is silenced by Muhammad because Malcolm disobeyed Muhammad's orders that no minister should make any comments about President Kennedy's death.

1964 By March 1, Malcolm's relationship with Muhammad is strained further because of Muhammad's silencing of Malcolm and also because of rumors that Muhammad has forbidden other Muslims from communicating with Malcolm.

On March 8, Malcolm X issues a press statement in which he announces his departure from the NOI—a move that stuns Muhammad, who at the time is living in Phoenix. As part of the break, Malcolm establishes the Organization of Afro-American Unity-Muslim Mosque, Inc.

On March 17, officials of NOI request that Malcolm return to NOI the organization's property in his possession, including the house and the car he is using.

On March 19, Malcolm broadens conflict between himself and the NOI by airing the dispute in a press conference.

On March 26, Malcolm X has an impromptu meeting with Rev. Martin Luther King, Jr., in the U.S. capitol after they observe the Senate filibuster over the Civil Rights Bill.

In April, Malcolm travels to Germany, Mecca, Saudi Arabia, Beirut, Cairo, Nigeria, Ghana, Liberia, Senegal, and Morocco. While in Mecca, he performs the Islamic Haj to acquire the *Hajj* (*or Alhaji*) title.

In late May, Malcolm returns to New York and continues to debate and give speeches around the country.

At the end of May, his Muslim Mosque sponsors a forum at the Audubon Ballroom in New York. Malcolm indicates that his split with Muhammad involved Muhammad's adultery and fathering of six illegitimate children.

In June, Malcolm calls the Civil Rights Bill a farce and discusses the Organization of Afro-American Unity (OAAU) as a group that he has organized to do "whatever necessary to bring the Negro struggle from the level of civil rights to the level of human rights."

In July, Malcolm sends to the *New York Post* as well as distributes an open letter to Muhammad, the NOI leader, calling for an end to the hostilities between them.

In July, Malcolm flies to Cairo, Egypt, to attend Organization of African Unity annual meeting.

In early August, Malcolm reports several acts of attempted violence and threats on his life to New York police authorities.

In September, ruling on the eviction notice filed by the NOI, a New York judge orders Malcolm and his family to vacate the East Elmhurst property by January 31, 1965.

In November, Malcolm X travels to Oxford, where he takes part in a debate of the Oxford Union at University of Oxford—a successful event which made Oxford students have a lot of respect for Malcolm X.

In early December, Malcolm returns to the United States and gives a major speech at Harvard University.

In mid-December, Louis Walcott, who later becomes Louis Farrakhan, writes an article in *Muhammad Speaks,* in which he implies that Malcolm X is worthy of death.

In December, Malcolm and Betty's fourth daughter, Gamilah (or Gumilah), is born.

1965　In the New Year, Malcolm speaks to SNCC students who visit Harlem and speaks at OAAU rallies, radio shows in New York, New Hampshire, and television shows in Canada.

In mid-January, Malcolm travels to Selma where SNCC is mobilizing voting rights and speaks at Brown's Chapel AME Church.

In late January, Malcolm travels to London and attempts to travel to Paris, but he is denied entry into Paris by the French government.

In early February, Malcolm's house is firebombed. Later that month, his family is evicted from the home.

In mid-February, in a conversation with Alex Haley, Malcolm X expresses concerns that the violence threats and incidents may be instigated by people other than the Muslims.

On February 21, Malcolm X is assassinated at an OAAU Rally at the Audubon Ballroom. He is pronounced dead on arrival at Columbia Presbyterian Hospital.

On February 22, Martin Luther King sends a telegram to Betty Shabazz to express his sadness and grief over Malcolm's death.

On February 23, Norman 3X Butler is arrested as one of the suspects in Malcolm's murder.

On February 27, Malcolm's funeral takes place at Faith Temple Church of God in Christ in New York. Ossie Davis, a close family friend, gives the eulogy. Malcolm is buried at Ferncliff Cemetery in Hartsdale, New York, with Attorney Sutton's help in obtaining a burial plot.

Posthumously, *The Autobiography of Malcolm X*, written in collaboration with Alex Haley (famous author of *Roots*), is published.

Also, posthumously, Betty Shabazz—pregnant when Malcolm X was assassinated—gives birth to twin daughters who are named in Malcolm X's honor as Malaak and Malikah.

In March, Malcolm's widow Betty Shabazz travels to Mecca to perform the Islamic *Hajj* pilgrimage, similar to what her late husband (Malcolm) did, which she performs in honor of her assassinated husband.

1966   After court motions and relevant delays, Malcolm's murder trial, which began in 1966, ends a few months later for Thomas Hagan, who admits his role in the killing, to be sentenced to 20 years to life imprisonment. The two accomplices are also found guilty and jailed.

1975   NOI leader, the Honorable Elijah Muhammad, dies.

        In July, Betty Shabazz earns her doctoral (Ed.D.) degree from the University of Massachusetts at Amherst, Massachusetts. A year before (1974), as part of her graduate study experience, Betty was inducted into the Delta Sigma Theta sorority.

1978   Louis Farrakhan takes over as leader of the NOI to succeed the Honorable Elijah Muhammad.

1992   Gregory Reed, a collector of manuscripts and art, purchases the original manuscript of Malcolm X for $100,000 at the auction of the estate of Alex Haley, who collaborated with Malcolm X in writing his 1965 autobiography.

        In January, the FBI accuses Malcolm's daughter Quibilah of conspiring to kill Louis Farrakhan, who the family holds responsible for creating the environment that led to Malcolm's assassination.

1995   In May, the charges against Quibilah, Malcolm X's daughter, are to be dropped if she agrees to undergo treatment for chemical dependency and avoid any other crimes.

1997   On June 23, Betty Shabazz—born on May 28, 1934, at Pinehurst, Georgia—dies in a fire accident that was allegedly triggered in her Bronx home by her then 12-year-old grandson, Malcolm, named for her husband Malcolm X. Malcolm is the son of Qubilah, who was charged in 1995 for conspiring to kill Louis Farrakhan.

2011   Columbia University professor Manning Marable's monumental 594-page biography of Malcolm, titled *A Life of Reinvention: Malcolm X*, is published to an uproar by Malcolm X's children because of part of the contents.

In March, Thomas Hagan, who spent 45 years in jail for confessing to the assassination, is paroled in New York at the age of 69. He does express regret for his involvement in the assassination. The two other convicted killers, who never confessed to the assassination, were paroled several years ago.

2013   Malcolm X's grandson, Malcolm Shabazz, is killed in a nightclub brawl in Mexico City, Mexico. The family of Malcolm X, in a statement, writes that young Malcolm is now re-united, in death, with his grandfather (Malcolm X) and great grandfather (Earl Little).

Chapter 1

THE EARLY YEARS

Malcolm Little, the man that the world has come to know as Malcolm X, has a fascinating family history that he himself used to tell outsiders. He learned from his mother that when she was pregnant, hooded riders of the Ku Klux Klan (KKK), the white supremacist and racist group, came to their Omaha, Nebraska, home to look for Malcolm's father, the Reverend Earl Little. Opening the door in such a way that the Klansmen could see her big belly, Mrs. Little told them that her husband was off on a preaching trip out of town. According to Malcolm, who wrote about it later, the Klansmen made threats as well as warnings at his pregnant mother. They told her that her family needed to get out of town because her husband's preaching about going "back to Africa" was causing trouble. The Klan did not want Malcolm's father spreading information about Marcus Garvey, the black Nationalist leader, whom Malcolm's father revered and followed.[1]

It was during a time of great racial and political upheaval in the United States and abroad when Malcolm X was born on May 19, 1925, to Louise Norton and Earl Little, Christian activist parents. By the time Malcolm was born, Earl and Louise already had three older children: Wilfred was the eldest child, followed by a sister named Hilda, and a brother named Philbert. In addition to the children that Earl had with Louise, he had three older children with a previous wife, whom he left before marrying Malcolm's mother. Malcolm's father, popularly known as Rev. Earl, was tall but on the heavy side, and had a dark complexion. In contrast, his mother had lighter skin and was slim. Although her Grenadian mother was a black woman, Louise's father was a white Scottish man, whom she never met.

It was not surprising then that Malcolm's appearance was somewhat of a mix between both of his parents. For example, his eyes were bluish and greenish and his hair was reddish brown, both of which were uncommon for a black child.

As a youngster, Malcolm's view of the world would be influenced by his parents' social backgrounds, experiences, and the political issues that prevailed during his day. As Malcolm later wrote in his autobiography: "All of our experiences fuse into our personality. Everything that happened to us is an ingredient."[2]

The time of Malcolm X's birth was marked by blatant racial discrimination and oppression against blacks. It was a time when blacks and whites in the United States lived separate and unequal lives. They did not live in the same neighborhoods or work in the same places. Black school children did not use new books, but only the old books that were discarded after they were used by white children. Racial slurs, racial prejudice, and racial violence were accepted and lawful. That meant that white people regularly called blacks "niggers" and they harassed and intimidated them without any punishment from the law. As a result, blacks were forced to attend separate and inferior educational institutions, as they were not allowed to attend most colleges and universities of their choice. Also, blacks were barred from holding jobs in many professions, and they were not allowed to go to the polls to cast their votes at legislative and presidential elections until voting rights laws were passed.

Young Malcolm was born into a world that was marked by racial violence. Murders were commonplace during Malcolm's childhood. Unlike today, blacks often had no legal recourse to defend themselves. Lynching, a process whereby black men and women were hung from trees after being beaten, shot, or castrated, was prevalent and widespread. The statistics of black lynching are staggering; for example, between the year that Malcolm's parents were married in 1919 and 1925, a period of only five years, almost 2,000 blacks were reported to have been lynched. In fact, an author pointed out how a mere accusation of a black man raping a white woman could lead to the instant lynching of the accused, as the author described lynchings as "acts of hatred and violence."[3] Racial violence was so high that, apart from the rampant acts of lynching, there were 26 race riots that occurred in the "red summer" of 1919 in American cities in both the country's North and the South.

During the same decade, only three years before Malcolm was born, a race riot in Tulsa, Oklahoma, resulted in over 100 people being killed and 11,000 blacks being left homeless when their segregated neighborhoods were leveled by bombs that whites used to drive them out of the city. The Ku Klux Klan was so active during the decade in which Malcolm X was born that the governor of Oklahoma in 1923 declared the state to be in a "state of rebellion and insurrection" as a result of widespread Klan activities.

Transparent or graphic change was equally important during the decade that Malcolm was born. Therefore, during the early 1900s, millions of African Americans migrated from the Deep South to northern states like Michigan and Wisconsin, where Malcolm spent some of his years as a youngster.

The black migration movement created the communities that Malcolm X spent time in, traveled in, and spoke to as he worked and organized as an adult. The movement to cities was precipitated by the industrial revolution and the fact that, after World War I, the United States was one of the world's largest manufacturing countries. Blacks and whites alike poured into the cities, but problems occurred because cities were not structured to handle the ensuing crowding and also because there were not enough jobs to go around. There was also not enough housing for the new migrants. In a society where whites dominated often through violence and the use of unfair laws, blacks were often forced to live in ghettos, and they struggled to find and keep jobs. Malcolm's parents, like most blacks who lived in cities, faced these dilemmas and, later in life, Malcolm faced them as well.

Yet, despite the prevailing discrimination and violence, Americans yearning for freedom in the face of obstacles either survived or shined through them. Such freedom expressed itself through the works of the artists, writers, and musicians of the Harlem Renaissance, that era, in Nell Irvin Painter's words, of "black cultural flowering in New York City in the 1920s." Black artists and writers of the Harlem Renaissance included Countee Cullen, Mamie Smith, Langston Hughes, Duke Ellington, W. E. B. Du Bois, Richard Wright, and the brothers J. Rosamond and James Weldon Johnson, who wrote the song "Lift Every Voice and Sing," later popularized as the "Negro National Anthem."

Apart from the Harlem Renaissance of the 1920s, blacks were also especially active in organizational efforts that resisted racial discrimination and outright segregation almost two decades earlier. That was why in 1905, for example, the Niagara Movement came into existence for the founding of the National Association for the Advancement of Colored People (NAACP) as well as that of the Urban League, two black survivalist organizations led by radical black leaders like Dr. Du Bois and others. Around the same time, in the 1920s, Andrew Foster organized the National Negro League, which was composed of six teams from midwestern cities that had large African American populations. These organizational efforts set the stage for the civil rights movement of the 1960s to which Malcolm X contributed immensely through his provocative rhetoric, travels, and writings, including the completion of his only known memoirs, co-authored with Alex Haley of *Roots* fame.

FOUNDATIONAL INFLUENCES ON MALCOLM'S EARLY LIFE

Especially crucial to Malcolm's later work was the burgeoning of African American political organizations. In terms of foundational influences, one of the most important was the Universal Negro Improvement Association (UNIA), which was established by Marcus Garvey in 1914 in Jamaica, but Garvey moved to the United States in 1916 to establish a Harlem chapter with additional 30 chapters organized in cities with large black populations like Omaha, where Malcolm's parents lived. The UNIA's main objective was to promote black pride and the need for blacks to see Africa as their ancestral home, where they could move to and live. Malcolm's parents were members of the UNIA and, as a result, they believed fervently in Marcus Garvey's message of black pride and his ultimate back-to-Africa movement. It was their way of fighting against the racial violence, racial segregation, and racial injustices that were a part of their daily experiences.

There were a lot of historic happenings prior to Malcolm's birth in 1925. It was in that same year that A. Philip Randolph organized the Brotherhood of Sleeping Car Porters, which was an organization with union status for black men, who worked as porters on the sleeping cars of the railroad. In fact, railroad jobs were not as difficult for black men to get but they had little say in what they were paid and how they were treated. It took Randolph and his black associates not less than 12 years to get legal rights to bargain on behalf of the members of their association, but in the interim, Randolph used his influence to make sure that black workers were treated fairly and paid more respectable wages than they had been given in the past. His efforts not only led to improvements for black sleeping car porters, but catalyzed and energized other blacks as well.

Malcolm's parents were convinced that Garvey's philosophies were important to the improvement of black people. Additionally, Garvey preached a message of economic independence for blacks as the only way to rid themselves of their dependence on whites. Furthermore, Garvey argued that black people needed their own jobs, their own schools, and their own spiritual and ancestral home in Africa. Garvey's philosophy was seen as a message of hope and independence, which resonated well with Earl Little and Louise Norton Little, Malcolm's parents. It was, therefore, not surprising that in 1923, Earl Little became the head of a chapter of the UNIA in Omaha, Nebraska.

Earl's UNIA affiliation did not seem to have economic value. Therefore, due to Earl's poor economic circumstances, life was hard for the Little family in which Malcolm had been born in 1925. That was compounded by racial discrimination, which did not provide blacks with opportunities to get education or skills needed to hold high-paying jobs. In fact, Malcolm's father himself did not have much schooling. Unable to find a stable job, he worked as an itinerant Baptist preacher, which meant that he did not have a regular salary but lived off what he was given in Baptist churches as a "love offering," which was a small monetary compensation given for his preaching on Sundays in different churches.

In contrast to the background of Earl, Malcolm's mother, Louise, had a higher educational training from her native Grenada, thereby encouraging her children to study hard in school and make something of themselves. However, as a woman and a mother of young children, her opportunities to work outside of the home were limited, especially when Earl was alive. The family also earned a small income, in the form of an allowance, from Earl's work as president of the local branch of the UNIA movement, headed internationally by Garvey. However, that work was both short-term and limited. Still, due to their relatively limited education and lack of access to steady employment, Earl, Louise, and their children, including young Malcolm at this time, lived a hand-to-mouth existence.

It was known in the community that Malcolm's father and mother were avid supporters of the UNIA, and that was why Earl Little spoke out frequently about the rights of black people, a mantra that he had learned from some of the rhetorical speeches and even publications of the UNIA leader, Garvey. Since he also served as a Baptist preacher, Earl often used the pulpit as a forum to discuss the UNIA and his views that black people should join the movement and live by its principles. Although Malcolm was a young child at the time, Earl Little reportedly brought his youngest child to the UNIA meetings, where Malcolm heard his father preach the gospel of Christ as well as the good news of black pride, espoused mainly by the UNIA leadership. In 1923, Marcus Garvey was arrested for mail fraud, wire fraud, and other alleged fraudulent practices in connection with the way he collected funds for UNIA work. In 1924, he was convicted, and in 1925, Garvey's appeal against his conviction failed, and he had to serve two years in federal prison, subject to his deportation later to his native Jamaica.[4]

Earl Little still continued to encourage black people, as Garvey did, to have pride in their race and to seek economic independence, just as was being preached by the UNIA as a radical black movement. Reportedly, Earl also wrote letters to the president of the United States to plead for Garvey's freedom and his release from detention while his case was being determined by the American legal system. At this time, Malcolm was very young, and his family moved around a lot, due in part to the search for work that would help the Little family make ends meet as well as a result of Earl Little's work with the UNIA. For example, the family moved in 1929 from Omaha to Milwaukee, Wisconsin, where Earl worked with the UNIA on a semi-full-time basis. From there, they moved a year later to Albion, Michigan, and then, in 1930, to the outskirts of Lansing, Michigan, where Malcolm's youngest sister, Yvonne, was born in 1931.

When in Lansing, the Littles used the money that they managed to save to purchase a modest home situated in the outskirts of the town. The neighborhood that the Little family moved into was predominantly white and, as a result, some of the white residents engaged in a number of tactics to force them to move from there. When Mr. Little made it clear that he and his family planned to stay in the neighborhood, the house was burned to the ground by an arsonist in 1932, when Malcolm's baby sister Yvonne was barely a year old. While the house was on fire, the local fire department reportedly came to the scene to see what was going on, yet Malcolm and his family were unable to convince the fire officials, as expected, to assist them in their efforts to save their house. After this incident, the family was then forced to move two additional times in Michigan in an effort to avoid racial violence. For young Malcolm and his family, racial violence was an ever-present issue that they seemed unable to escape.

Despite his family's problems, however, Malcolm frequently observed his father being engaged in organizational efforts and community service regarding black pride and lifting up the black race. Mr. Little was not deterred by threats of violence against him or his family, and he continued to work indefatigably to convince blacks of their rights and to fight against racial subordination. By 1931, Malcolm was enrolled in kindergarten at Pleasant Grove Elementary School in the outskirts of Lansing, Michigan, and he was also a frequent traveler with his father, as the latter organized for the Garvey cause. However, Earl's fight against racial violence came to a stunning end as a result of a freak accident when Malcolm was just six years old. On September 28, 1931, Malcolm was awakened in the middle of the night to find his mother screaming, while police officers were trying to calm her down. He later learned that his mother was in tears because Earl had been found dead near a trolley track. The circumstances surrounding Earl Little's death were strange because it appeared at the time that he had fallen underneath the wheels of the trolley vehicle, but no one remembered seeing him near the trolley.

Subsequently, Louise told Malcolm and her other children that Earl had been surreptitiously killed by white people, who did not want him in the neighborhood to organize blacks and also to encourage what he called black or racial pride. In fact, the way the mother reported the death to her children was so crude that it would make a poor impression on young Malcolm and his siblings; instead of finding another adult to explain the circumstances of the death to her children, Mrs. Little simply told them that their father was dead, and that they were to be on their own from that time. Also, the local police promised to investigate the murder, but no arrests were ever made in Earl Little's death. While Earl and his sad death may have been forgotten by the police, he had made an indelible impact, as a father, on young Malcolm, which would later become evident in the speeches about black pride and independence that Malcolm made throughout the world.

Earl Little's death created a huge vacuum in Malcolm's family. Louise was forced to fend for herself and her seven children during a time of extreme poverty and depression. To ensure a brighter future for the family, Louise continued to send her children to school as she looked for new ways to put food on the table, clothes on their backs, and a roof over their heads. Soon, Louise found work as a part-time domestic worker for some local white families. Her duties required that she was to cook, clean, and do the laundry in exchange for a small sum of money that was usually between 50 cents and a dollar for a day of work. This was often not enough money for the family to eat, but Malcolm and his siblings did odd jobs to raise funds as well as to hunt in an effort to get food to eat. A blessing to the family at the time was when, eventually, Malcolm's mother began to receive a welfare check on a regular basis. This was during the Great Depression in America in the 1930s, when President Franklin D. Roosevelt's government had established welfare places, where needy Americans could get food and commodities for their families. In exchange for the small pittance, people who received welfare from the government were subject to visits by social workers to investigate their circumstances.

During this time, Malcolm continued to attend school at Pleasant Grove Elementary School. His fourth-grade picture, taken in 1937, depicts him in a group of all white children, with Malcolm being the only person of color in the group. While some of his classmates played with him and treated him well, he was often the butt of ridicule and jokes because of the color of his skin. However, unlike his other classmates at Pleasant Grove Elementary School, Malcolm had the additional burden of ensuring that he did not do anything that would engender violence against him. As a young black man, especially one without a father, he could be susceptible to threats and violence from other white children and their parents. According to most accounts, Malcolm was a bright child, who not only excelled in his school work, but also did exceptionally well in athletics. He always strove to do his best even under difficult circumstances.

Louise severely suffered from the hardship of life at the time. Aside from the fact that she was a widow with seven children to care for, she also had to contend with extreme poverty, racism, and the disrespect of the social workers, who often arrived unannounced at Malcolm's house for purposes of inspection. All of these matters began to take a toll on his mother. Soon, she began to show signs of what Malcolm would later recognize as mental illness. It included the fact that Louise began to talk to herself as well as to ignore her children's conversations and their daily needs. She also cried for long periods of time and often showed signs of depression. Still aware of her circumstances, Malcolm's mother objected to the condescending treatment that most of the social workers meted out to her and her children. She resented their intrusion on her life and their meddling into her rights as a parent. By 1939, almost eight years after the death of her husband, Louise was declared legally insane and committed to a mental institution, where she lived for over two decades. Twelve-year-old Malcolm and his younger siblings soon became wards of the state. At the time, young Malcolm had experienced more pain and loss than most adults experience in a lifetime.

Life as a ward of the state was not easy because it meant that Malcolm and his six siblings had to leave home and remain separated from one another in order to live with people that they did not know—indeed, total strangers. During this time, Malcolm stayed in foster homes and in juvenile homes, never finding a family that provided the kind of environment, love, and security that had eluded him for so long.

It also meant that Malcolm was to be uprooted from Pleasant Grove Elementary School, which he had attended all of his life, in order to enroll in Lansing's West Junior High School. There, he had to become accustomed to a new setting, new teachers, and new friends. The records indicate that Malcolm was a bright student who did well in school. But there is also evidence that he was prone to engaging in pranks. As he had done at Pleasant Grove Elementary School, Malcolm also played basketball at West Junior High School. He continued to work hard and strive for excellence in both academics and athletics. However, it was during this period in his life that his hopes and dreams were dashed once again, this time, by a school teacher whom he admired and respected.

During a conversation about his career goals, Malcolm shared with his junior high school teacher his ambition to become a lawyer. According to Malcolm's published autobiography, the teacher informed him that black children could not work as lawyers, and that he should focus his dreams and aspirations toward something that he could do and was also either attainable or acceptable. In the end, it was shown that the teacher's assessment was definitely incorrect, as there were black lawyers as well as black students who, like Malcolm, were preparing for careers in law during this era. In fact, if not for the work of black attorneys, many of the favorable court decisions, including *Brown v. Board of Education*, which barred legal segregation in public schools and led to the undermining of segregation in all walks of American life, would not have been possible. However, Malcolm looked up to the teacher and internalized his perspectives as reality. For Malcolm, the teacher's admonitions regarding his chances in life were sacrosanct and it discouraged him from aspiring toward his dream of becoming a lawyer.

Around the same time, Ella, Malcolm's stepsister from his father's first marriage invited Malcolm to come to Boston and live with her. In February 1941, Malcolm moved to Boston, where he began a new life with Ella and her family. While Malcolm's classmates were preparing for high school, he was preparing for the next phase of his educational life in the school of "street life." He was just 14 years old.

As Malcolm prepared for his move to Boston, America was on the brink of World War II. In December of the same year that Malcolm moved to Boston, the Japanese attacked Pearl Harbor. Malcolm X and his classmates at his Boston High School were taught that an African American soldier aboard the naval ship called *West Virginia*, who heard the attack, pulled the ship's captain to safety and later used the ship's guns to succeed in shooting down four Japanese planes. Without intervention by the black sailor by the name of Dorrie Miller, many more American lives would have been lost that day. Until then, blacks too had played heroic roles in the war effort, yet their efforts were not publicly acknowledged until Miller's feat. The nonrecognition of black heroism prevented these soldiers from getting a fair share of the prevailing opportunities, including military and other honors issued for valor and selfless services in the Armed Forces of the United States. Mr. Miller was publicly recognized for his bravery against the invading Japanese air force armed personnel.

In fact, the *New York Times* reported on Thursday, July 15, 2010, that Vernon Baker, who died at the age of 90 that week, happened to be the only living black veteran awarded the Medal of Honor for valor in World War II, which he received 52 years after he wiped out four German machine-gun nests on a hilltop in the north of Italy. It was former president Bill Clinton who bestowed America's highest award for bravery on Mr. Baker at a White House ceremony on January 13, 1997—52 years later. At the ceremony, Mr. Baker, who was advanced in age at the time, said to President Clinton and the audience: "I was a soldier and I had a job to do."[5] Apart from the case of Mr. Baker given earlier, the New York–based newspaper reported that some military historians had given the U.S. Army the names of 10 other black servicemen who they felt should have also been awarded the Medal of Honor. Unfortunately, it was alleged that an Army Board for such honors deleted all references to the 10 men's race, and that in the end, the board agreed that only seven of these black men deserved to be cited for bravery above and beyond the call of duty; hence Mr. Baker was left out of the seven until 52 years later (in 1997), when former president Clinton honored him similarly. In fact, it was because of unfortunate instances like those of Mr. Baker and the seven other black servicemen who were to receive their honors for valor much after the fact, that Mr. A. Philip Randolph, a leading civil rights campaigner in the mid-1930s, organized a protest march of 100,000 blacks to protest the exclusion of fellow blacks from being honored in the defense industry. Mobilized by this important show of force, former president Franklin D. Roosevelt was prompted to issue Executive Order 8802, which prohibited employers from discriminating against blacks in this way during wartime. Since the presidential Executive Order did not affect employment, employers throughout the United States continued to hire whites only in this lucrative industry.[6]

It is ironic that in the 1930s, while blacks were being generally discriminated against in terms of employment, black soldiers were training in largely-segregated conditions to defeat the enemies of the United States in wars. Among the many heroic efforts of such black veterans were the Tuskegee Airmen, who successfully escorted white bombers all over Europe without losing a single flyer, while also destroying or damaging over 400 enemy airplanes. It is important to note that young Malcolm was coming of age at the time of the foregoing important transitions in the black communities, including the racism that his fellow blacks in the Army were faced with. However, unlike their roles in World War I, when blacks were merely content to fight and be included in various military divisions, black men and women in the 1940s, including World War II period, demanded more. That was why they were unwilling to accept life in the country of their birth that cared more about victory abroad than ending racial violence and discrimination at home. For example, there was a clear-cut aggressiveness in the Boston area, in which Malcolm lived, which did influence his own outlook on life. Furthermore, the atmosphere gave birth to a black wartime culture, in which zoot suits, conks, and the lindy hop had significant meaning during the times and also as rites of passage in Malcolm's young life.

THE SCHOOL OF STREET LIFE AND HARD KNOCKS FOR MALCOLM

By the age of 14, young Malcolm's education had taken a new path and it took place in a different context. Previously, he had been formally enrolled in traditional schools, going from kindergarten to junior high school in predominantly-white, small-town settings. His education at Pleasant Grove and Mason, for example, involved white teachers, bucolic buildings, and traditional homework assignments. Most of his friends were white as were members of the larger community. Moreover, the pace of life was slow and calm.

By contrast, Malcolm's educational experiences in Boston were anything but formal. His new classrooms were the local streets, bars, pool halls, and nightlife of Boston. His classmates were the new friends that he made on the streets, many of whom his sister Ella asked him to avoid because of their known or suspected bad character. His new homework sadly included figuring out how to hustle and make it in a city that was as different from Lansing, Michigan, as day is from night. Therefore, all of Malcolm's education occurred in cities, which had a sizeable and growing population of his fellow blacks, who had lived in the city for decades. To Malcolm's delight, black people in Boston had their own community called Roxbury, where the well-to-do as well as the outright hustlers had the goal of making a better life for themselves. Being a part of that world at the time, Malcolm was prepared to excel in learning how to make it on his own.

The Boston area of Roxbury, where Malcolm and his sister lived, was seen as the seat of black culture in the city, as it had a history of its own, and it was initially one of the first black-populated areas established in the Massachusetts Bay Colony in 1630. Prior to the settlement of blacks in the area, Roxbury was the home of industry and also to previous groups of white immigrants. The racial composition of the neighborhood changed as a result of migration of blacks from the American south to northern cities in search of racial freedom and economic opportunity. The neighborhood boasted black professionals, whose families had been longtime residents of Boston. It also contained a new crop of southern-born black folks, who lived, in some ways, at tension with their Southern past and their new black neighbors.

Like many of the other new transplants or residents, Malcolm tried hard during his teenage years to fit in, and the easiest way for him to succeed in this regard was to connect with other young men on the streets. In his autobiography, Malcolm humorously described his arrival in Boston. Among other details, he recounted in the book that he looked like a Li'l Abner, and that it was the time that he had kinky reddish hair, which was cut hick style, and that he failed to use grease in the hair. During this time, Malcolm sometimes had a green suit, and the coat sleeves stopped above his wrists, while his pants legs showed three inches of socks. Malcolm's three-quarter-length Lansing department store's topcoat seemed a much lighter green. Therefore, his appearance was too much even for his sister, Ella, who told Malcolm later that she had seen members of the Little family come up from rural Georgia in even worse shape than Malcolm was at the time. She said so as a consolation for the young Malcolm.[7]

In many respects, Ella was the parent that Malcolm missed during his formative childhood years. Seen by Malcolm as a "big, black and outspoken" woman, her home was a refuge for young and impressionistic Malcolm. He also found solace under the shadow of Ella's care. When he first moved to Boston, Ella insisted that he should take his time to look around the city but not rush to find a job. In following her directions, Malcolm first explored the affluent side of black life and, during his initial exploration, he saw the site where the black soldier by the name of Crispus Attucks became the first person to lose his life in the Revolutionary War, who also happened to be the first volunteered black soldier killed in the war.

After spending time on the city buses, Malcolm took a stroll in Cambridge and walked around the Harvard University area. Little did he know that in the near future, he would be invited to give a talk as part of a highly-respected forum of the Harvard University Law School. Taken together, the sights and sounds of the big city were invigorating for the young black teenager, who wrote later that he spent "the first month in town with my mouth hanging open" in amazement.[8]

Yet, Malcolm was not content to merely visit the genteel areas that Ella recommended. He yearned to see the underbelly of the city as well. These were the places that Ella referred to as the ghetto sections. Malcolm later wrote in his autobiography that the world of grocery stores as well as walk-up flats, cheap restaurants, poolrooms, bars, storefront churches, and pawnshops did hold for him what he saw as a natural allure.[9] Not long after young Malcolm felt that he had discovered and explored this part of Boston well, he met Shorty, who became his primary teacher and confidant. Their initial meeting took place as Malcolm stood outside the pool hall, where Shorty worked as an aspiring musician, who was, on this occasion, working in his spare time to play the saxophone.

During their initial conversations, Shorty realized that he and Malcolm were from the same town of Mason, Michigan, which made them home boys. From that time on, Shorty took Malcolm under his wing and taught him everything that he knew, and Shorty was the first person to talk to Malcolm about "playing the numbers," an illegal activity that is similar to playing the modern-day lottery. For black people who mostly earned just enough money to survive, hitting the numbers was a way to move beyond the hand-to-mouth existence into a more secure lifestyle. However, Shorty was also very practical, as he helped Malcolm to find his first job in Boston. Back then, jobs were called slaves, and Shorty helped Malcolm to find a slave as a shoeshine boy, as Malcolm took over from a man named Freddie, who was quitting the job because he had hit the numbers. The shoeshine stand was outside the Roseland State Ballroom, which featured some of the most exciting dances in the city.

One of the first things that Malcolm had to learn how to do was shine shoes with the speed and alacrity necessary to survive in the big city. He learned this skill from Freddie, who not only taught him the trade, but also taught him how to make his shoes shine very well to the satisfaction of the owner of the shoes. Freddie also taught Malcolm how to engage black and white men differently so that he could earn tips. From his vantage point as a shoeshine boy, therefore, Malcolm had the opportunity to meet several important black people, including artists, who played in the ballroom, hear the latest news about the happenings in Boston and around the world, and perfect his craft.

Not long after he began his shoeshine job, Malcolm also became involved in gambling and betting games that used two types of dice together. While shooting craps, he had his first drink of alcohol, smoked his first cigarette, and smoked his first reefer joint (or marijuana). A reefer joint was made of dried marijuana leaves rolled up into a cigarette. For Malcolm, drinking and smoking made him appear to be more grown-up and more sophisticated than he really was. At the time, one of the important hallmarks of city life for young urban men was the zoot suit, and Malcolm longed for this attire. Zoot suits were tight-waisted and wide-legged, with tight-cuffed trousers. The coat was long, and had wide lapels and padded shoulders. They were worn especially by black men as well as Latinos, Italian American, and Asian American men during the late 1930s and early 1940s. The only thing that remained for Malcolm to feel totally integrated into city life was to get a "conk."

A conk was a hairstyle in which the hair is straightened with lye or other chemicals to relax the natural curls and make it straight. The lye agitates the skin while straightening the hair to the extent that the scalp feels like it is on fire. Depending on the texture of the hair, the lye or other chemical mix must stay on the hair longer to ensure that it is straightened. After several minutes of using it, all of the lye must be washed off to ensure that it does not permanently damage the scalp. In Malcolm's case, his first conk was administered by Shorty. In his autobiography, Malcolm recounted the experience, whereby he wrote that his eyes watered as well as his nose was running, and that he could "not stand it any longer; I bolted to the washbasin. I was cursing Shorty with every name I could think of when he got the spray going and started soap-lathering my head."[10] Eventually, however, Shorty got all of the chemicals out, and he had a head full of straightened hair that slicked back with grease. With his zoot suit, conk, and new behaviors of drinking, smoking, and shooting craps, Malcolm's education in street life was off to an accelerated pace. He had accomplished all of this before his 16th birthday.

Soon, Malcolm found a laboratory in which to try out his newfound street education, the party scene that Shorty introduced him to. Dressed like city boys, Malcolm and Shorty attended many of the parties, where they drank alcohol and smoked reefer. In this environment, Malcolm also learned to dance and once he caught the dancing fever, he found it too difficult to shine shoes near the Roseland Ballroom, while other folks were dancing. As a result, he quit his job as a shoeshine boy because it conflicted with his opportunity to dance. One of Malcolm's favorite dances was the lindy hop. It was named after Charles Lindbergh, the famous aviator. It is also known as the Jitterbug because of its smooth, rhythmic style, which involved two people who danced in rhythm to the music while also keeping pace with each other. Malcolm and his dance buddies partied hard and danced themselves into a frenzy, often moving to the music of Count Basie and other big bands.

As a guest in Ella's house, Malcolm did not stay unemployed very long. In fact, Ella worked hard to find Malcolm a job in the middle-class section of the city, where he could work among the upwardly-mobile segments of the black community. His job as a soda fountain clerk allowed him to work in a more serene environment. There, he met Laura, a black girl who was very smart but also very sheltered and protected by her elderly grandmother. Laura aspired to be a mathematician and she encouraged Malcolm to pursue his dream of becoming a lawyer. She came into the drugstore every day to buy a banana split, and she eventually became smitten with Malcolm. Although Laura's grandmother disapproved of Malcolm, Laura began to attend the late night dances with him. Laura was interested in proving to Malcolm that she was the best lindy hop partner. One night, however, a white woman named Sophie came into the Roseland Ballroom, where Malcolm and Laura were dancing. It was obvious to Malcolm that Sophie liked him. He liked Sophie too because of the way that she dressed and carried herself. He made the decision to take Laura home and return to the dance floor to be with Sophie.

Malcolm was 16 years old at the time, and being with Sophie made him feel like a million-dollar young man. Back in those days, the miscegenation laws made it illegal for black and white people to inter-marry. For Malcolm, therefore, Sophie was like a prize because he had something in her that black men were not supposed to have. He did not realize the awful impact that it had on Laura, who felt so hurt by Malcolm's rejection that she eventually became a prostitute and a drug addict. Furthermore, Malcolm liked Sophie because she bought things for him and paraded him around in her nice car. With Sophie's help, for example, Malcolm was able to move out of Ella's apartment and share Shorty's apartment. This move rendered Malcolm more accessible to Sophie, whom Ella did not like. In fact, Ella wanted Malcolm to pursue a relationship with Laura, whom she thought of as a nice girl that would help Malcolm settle down and live a good life. Since Sophie had destroyed Ella's dream of a lasting relationship between Malcolm and Laura, Ella had no use for Sophie and she did not approve of Malcolm's relationship with the white woman. That is one reason that Ella helped Malcolm find a job that would take him away from Boston but also expose him to life in New York City, a place that Malcolm longed to know.

Malcolm's new job entailed selling sandwiches and beverages on board the Yankee Clipper, a train from Boston to New York, a job that he performed every other day. More important than the money that he made, however, was the ability to see Harlem, a place that he recalled his father talking about with pride during his lifetime. Harlem was, in many respects, an important source of culture and history for blacks in America. It was originally settled by the Dutch who, in fact, named the place after the city of Haarlem in the Netherlands. It simply meant that the original white residents were replaced by different groups of white immigrants, who happened to be the Dutch. By the early 20th century, blacks slowly began to move into Harlem. At the time, racism in the United States linked black people to lower property values. As a result, blacks who moved into a neighborhood usually drove white people out because they either believed in the stereotypes or they did not want their property values to decline. Over time, whites moved out and Harlem slowly became the black metropolis of Malcolm's day, where a mixture of blacks from all social and economic strata lived together in close proximity.

While working on the railroad, Malcolm also held jobs as dishwasher not only on the New York lines but also in Washington, D.C. He was astounded, during his visits to Washington, to see the wonderful sites, but also because of the abject poverty in which blacks lived within the shadow of the White House.

No city, however, impressed Malcolm as much as New York did. He was taken in by the lights, sounds, sophistication, food, people, culture, and the rhythm of the place. He frequented Small's Paradise Bar, which was a famous hangout spot for black people during the 1940s and 1950s. He also visited the Apollo Theater, where musical and entertainment greats like Dizzy Gillespie, Billy Eckstine, Billie Holiday, Ella Fitzgerald, and Dinah Washington performed.

At this time, Malcolm worked his job as a sandwich man on the train during the day, and at night, he and his friends got drunk. During that time, he became more and more dependent on alcohol and smoking reefer, and it began to show at work, where he reportedly showed up half-drunk and half-high. However, Malcolm was so good at selling sandwiches that he kept his job for a long time, even though customers complained about his increasingly rude, brazen, and arrogant behavior. When the train returned to Boston, Malcolm reconnected with his Roxbury friends.

By the time Malcolm was 17, in 1942, he had lost his job on the railroad, due largely to his attitude and complaints from customers. However, he had made such a good impression on the employees and owners of Small's that he was offered a job there as a waiter. From that vantage point, he worked and was educated by the local residents about city life as well as black culture. In New York, therefore, Malcolm continued education that he began in Roxbury in the study of street life. Not only was he learning about the culture, but he was also soaking up information about pimping, gambling, armed robbery, hustling, dope, and stealing. Eventually, Malcolm became so much a part of Harlem life that the people there gave him the nickname "Detroit Red."

During his time in Harlem, Sophie continued her relationship with him even though she married a white man. Malcolm reasoned that although Sophie enjoyed being with him, she also wanted to have a comfortable life. Marrying the white man ensured that she would be taken care of financially, while continuing the relationship with Malcolm ensured that part of her romantic needs would be met. Malcolm's efforts to help a soldier get his romantic needs met resulted in him being arrested by the police, and therefore, being fired from his job. That is because servicemen, who had been on the warfront, were especially susceptible to being bamboozled or easily misled by street smarts like Malcolm, then known as Detroit Red. As a result, the owners of Small's Paradise Bar had instructed their employees never to use their bar as a place to hustle soldiers or any other customer. In the end, the soldier was actually a foil that was disguised to catch people who would otherwise take advantage of real soldiers. Malcolm was taken to the police station and detained for a couple of days. Upon his release from jail, he was invited to join a Harlem drug ring, which took him deeper into his street life education.

As a 17-year-old boy, Malcolm had transitioned from a respectable job of waiter at one of Harlem's classiest bars to the life of a drug dealer who sold marijuana. Sammy, a black man of West Indian descent, who was also a leader in Harlem's crime world, recruited Malcolm to sell drugs. He loaned Malcolm $20 to purchase his first supply of marijuana, which Malcolm sold at a profit and promptly repaid Sammy's money at the end of the evening. Every day, Malcolm reportedly netted about $50 which, in his words, "was a fortune for a 17-year-old Negro." Malcolm's success did not last long. Soon, the narcotics police identified him as a drug dealer and started searching him on the streets and also searching his apartment. After a while, he ran out of money and had to borrow money again from Sammy, just to buy the drugs or to eat. He was running out of options, and he needed to find a new hustle before he ended up in jail.

While in New York and Boston, Malcolm kept in touch with Ella and his siblings back in Lansing. His brother Wilfred had become a trade instructor at Wilberforce. Reginald, who came to visit Malcolm during Malcolm's drug-dealing days, worked in the merchant marines. Hilda and Philbert were still in Lansing. During his conversations with family members, Malcolm learned that he had been called to appear before the Draft Board, which meant that he could be drafted into the Armed Forces. Malcolm was scared to death of going to the raging war in Europe. As he put it in his autobiography, there were three things that he was scared of as a teenager: jail, a job, and the Army. Therefore, in response to the Draft Board's summons, Malcolm put on the wildest zoot suit that he owned and acted like he had lost his mind. He talked fast, danced, wiggled, and acted like a "Harlem jigaboo"—all in an effort to convince the examiners that he was unfit to serve in the Army. Malcolm was convincing and adjudged mentally unstable, and indeed, incapable of serving in any branch of the U.S. Armed Forces.

Eventually, Malcolm became a full-time hustler, whose *modus operandi* was small-time burglaries. In order to get the nerve to rob people, he used cocaine before each burglary and in order to refrain from getting nervous, he resorted to the use of cocaine and other drugs between the thefts. It was during this time in his life that Reginald, his younger brother, came to live with Malcolm in New York. From time to time,

Malcolm worked on small burglaries with Sammy until one day, a misunderstanding led Sammy to try to kill Malcolm.

Later, on, Malcolm and Sammy patched things up, but Malcolm never again trusted his pal, and he began to look for a new hustling spot. He found one in the numbers running business, this time working for a white man. Malcolm also had other jobs in Harlem, including working as part of a prostitution ring that supplied black women and black men, respectively, for white men and white women. Since the hustles were illegal, Malcolm was often on the run from the police so that he could stay out of jail. He was also on the run from other hustlers with whom he had a misunderstanding or had tried to cheat. On some occasions, they tried to kill him, but his friend Shorty from Roxbury drove to New York just in the nick of time to rescue him and bring him back to the safety of Boston.

When Shorty drove to New York to pick Malcolm up, he saved his life. While Ella and Shorty were happy to have Malcolm back in Roxbury, they were truly amazed and perplexed by the change that he had undergone. Ella was worried about Malcolm's lack of respect as well as profanity, and she worried that he was on a steep decline toward serious trouble. Shorty, who had introduced him to hustling,

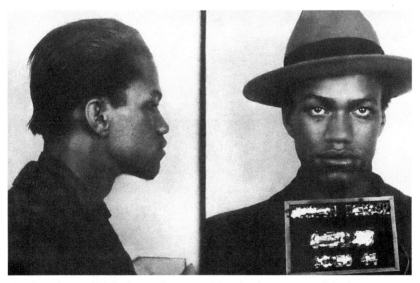

A police photo of Malcolm Little, at age 18, after being arrested for larceny in Boston, Massachusetts, in 1944. (© Bettmann/Corbis)

drinking, and smoking reefer, was also amazed at how much of the drugs Malcolm used and his dependence on harder drugs. Sophie, who continued to see Malcolm at Shorty's apartment, where Malcolm now lived, experienced a harder-edged Malcolm, who often requested larger sums of money and more favors from her than he had in the past. Malcolm used the first few weeks in Roxbury to sleep and get reacclimated to his environment. Not long after that initial period, however, he began working on a new hustle, one that he and Shorty could do together. He decided to form a burglary ring, whereby they were to rob rich whites in the Boston area, sell the property, and live off the profits.

For a while, the burglary ring to which Malcolm belonged worked well and they did not get caught. From the proceeds of the burglaries, Malcolm and his co-conspirators dressed well. They, in fact, used part of the proceeds of their burglary profits to entertain themselves in the best places. Then, like a bad dream, several problems converged on Malcolm at once and he was almost killed by the police as well as by Sophie's husband, who found out that Malcolm had been having an affair with his wife. Sophie's husband threatened to kill Malcolm. In this sense, Malcolm's arrest by the police on an unrelated charge was very much a blessing in disguise because it saved him from certain death for his adulterous behavior. At this point, Malcolm was 19 years of age, and the education in street life had ended with a detour to jail.

Chapter 2

IMPRISONMENT
AND EMBRACING ISLAM

Malcolm Little's 1944 arrest was as a result of a complaint filed against him by his own half-sister, Ella. The reason for the complaint and the subsequent arrest surprised Malcolm's other family members as well as his close friends because Malcolm had promised all of them that he was turning over a new leaf. At the time, Malcolm was working for a small salary at the local Sears Roebuck warehouse. Since his daily chores at his Sears work required a lot of physical labor, Malcolm quit the $20-a-week job. But being in a desperate need for money, Malcolm stole a fur coat belonging to Grace, who was Ella's sister and Malcolm's other half-sister. Malcolm sold the coat at a local pawn shop for $5. Outraged by the theft, Ella reported 19-year-old Malcolm Little to the local police, and he was promptly arrested and charged with theft. Since that was Malcolm's first arrest that led to a charge, a Roxbury court convicted him but simply let him go after imposing a suspended sentence of three months as well as a year's probation for Malcolm to be on good behavior.[1]

After the court ordeal, Malcolm decided to look for a new job anywhere that one was available. That was when Abe Goldstein, who was a friend of Ella, promised to assist Malcolm in his job search. Goldstein owned several businesses, including the Lobster Pond nightclub in New York. Malcolm accepted the job offer in the fall of 1944 and started to work for Goldstein in his nightclub. By January 1945, Malcolm had saved a few hundred dollars. As a result, he decided to leave New York to return to Roxbury, where he had also been sending a little part of his monthly salary to Ella and also to Reginald, one of his two older brothers. Back in Roxbury with Ella, Malcolm sought and found a job at the local Coral Gables bar. To earn additional money, Malcolm accepted a second job as a part-time busboy at the local Mayfair Ballroom.[2]

Soon, it became apparent that Malcolm took the two jobs as a cover for the petty crimes in which he was involved. One day, he decided to travel to Detroit and, while there, he robbed at gunpoint a fellow black man by the name of Douglas Haynes. It was in mid-March 1945, a few months short of Malcolm's 20th birthday on May 19. Haynes initially filed a complaint against Malcolm with the Detroit Police Department, and they alerted the East Lansing police that they were looking for Malcolm. It was on March 11, 1945, that Malcolm was arrested in East Lansing and was transported to the Detroit Police authorities. They charged him with grand larceny and required a bond payment of $1,000. Malcolm's brother Wilfred paid the bond, and Malcolm was once again a free man. With time on his hands, he decided to look for a new job. Soon, he found a position at a Lansing mattress-manufacturing company and a part-time job at a truck factory.[3]

When Malcolm's case came up in court, the presiding judge postponed its hearing to another date, after which Malcolm decided to leave town with the intention of forgetting about the upcoming trial. When he did not show up in court on the appointed day, a warrant was issued by the judge for his arrest, but it was not until almost a year later, in 1946, that Malcolm was arrested. At the time, Malcolm was working as a butler and occasional houseworker for Mr. Paul Lennon, an affluent local white man. Expecting Mr. Lennon to come to his assistance, Malcolm gave the man's name and residential particulars to the police when he was picked up. In the end, Malcolm was surprised that Lennon, his employer, did not show up to offer any assistance to him.[4]

Malcolm was still on the run from the law for the Haynes robbery charge. That was why he avoided living in either Detroit or Lansing. Instead, he chose to go and live in New York. Still, Malcolm was worried because he knew that if he were picked up for any legal infraction, he could be in serious trouble with the law. After all, the Michigan authorities had a warrant out for his arrest and he was also wanted for a parole violation in Massachusetts. Therefore, Malcolm had to avoid any trouble and be very careful.[5]

When Malcolm decided to return to Roxbury from New York, he had nowhere to stay. Once again, Ella came to his rescue and allowed him to stay with her. Unfortunately, Malcolm could not stay away from criminal mischief. After moving in with Ella, Malcolm started to work with a gang of petty thieves. These young men specialized in breaking into homes, looting clothes, watches, and other personal effects. Then, they would resell the stolen goods. At the time, Malcolm gave an expensive watch to a relative as a Christmas gift. Looking for money, the relative in turn sold the watch to a Boston jeweler, who suspected that the valuable watch was stolen. The jeweler informed the local police about the watch he had purchased from Malcolm's relative. When one of the watches that Malcolm had stolen from a burglary had a problem, he took the watch to the same jeweler, who tipped off the police the second time. When Malcolm returned for the watch, a policeman was waiting to arrest him. During his arrest, the police found on him a loaded .32 caliber pistol.

Right after his arrest, the police encouraged Malcolm to provide information about the other thieves that he worked with in exchange for a less serious charge that would not include the illegal possession of a weapon. Although the deal fell through, Malcolm appeared in court on only the larceny charges for the two stolen watches, and that was also the time that his friend Shorty Jarvis was picked up and brought to court for the same offense. Eventually, Malcolm and his friend did plead guilty at a Middlesex County courtroom to their charged offenses. Subsequently, Malcolm Little and Jarvis were convicted for their crimes and, due to their previous criminal backgrounds, both men were "sentenced to four concurrent eight-to-ten-year sentences, to be served in prison." Since both men pleaded guilty, there was no room for any appeal.

Malcolm and Jarvis began serving their imprisonment in Charlestown State Prison, one of the oldest prisons in the state of Massachusetts. Malcolm stayed in that prison for a year, but his sister Ella appealed to the prison authorities for Malcolm's transfer to another prison facility closer to Ella's home so that she could visit him more frequently. Deemed a model prisoner, Malcolm Little was transferred in 1948 to Norfolk Prison Colony, where he would learn from some of his relatives about the Honorable Elijah Muhammad and the black Muslim group known as the Nation of Islam (NOI). At the same time, Muhammad had also heard about Malcolm from two of Malcolm's older brothers, Philbert and Reginald, who had joined the NOI in the early 1940s. They planned to introduce NOI's Islamic teachings and principles to Malcolm.[6]

When Malcolm was still in prison, Philbert and Reginald gave him the mailing address of their mentor, the Honorable Elijah Muhammad. The main reason was that, upon his future release from jail, Malcolm's brothers wanted to help him turn his life around in order to avoid any more legal problems and imprisonment. With his brothers' encouragement, Malcolm started to communicate from his prison cell with the Honorable Elijah Muhammad. In his autobiography, Malcolm confirmed that, in desperation, he wrote to Muhammad not less than 25 times before formally leaving prison and joining the NOI. Apart from Muhammad being impressed with the eloquent manner in which Malcolm wrote to him, the imprisoned young man also found a way to explain in their correspondence that he wrote those letters to indicate his familiarity with the founder and leader of the NOI. Also, Malcolm wanted to show the NOI leader that he had done his homework about him. To impress Muhammad further, Malcolm Little informed him that although he did not live in Chicago, he still knew that the Honorable Elijah Muhammad, in fact, lived at 6116 South Michigan Avenue in Chicago, which was different from the general NOI mailing address to which he sent his letters.[7]

Although Muhammad, at that time, knew of Malcolm only through the letters they exchanged and brief discussions with his two older brothers, there would be a future opportunity for them to meet face-to-face, once he was released from prison. At the time that Malcolm was writing his many letters to the NOI leader, he had only a formal eighth-grade education. Because of Malcolm's limited education, Philbert and Reginald realized that his conversion to Islam would be a saving grace and an asset as it would give Malcolm something constructive to focus on and do when he was out of prison. That was why Malcolm's two brothers wanted to make sure that he would become actively affiliated with the NOI, which could help him to better himself through its private educational programs and rigid moral training to be able to avoid smoking, womanizing, and other social evils. Consequently, while still at the Norfolk Prison Colony in Massachusetts, Malcolm Little's two brothers, who were staunch NOI members in Detroit, were helping him to know about NOI rules and regulations. They wanted to prepare him to meet the Honorable Elijah Muhammad in person when he was released from prison. Encouraged by his brothers, Malcolm gave up cigarette smoking and the eating of pork. NOI founder Muhammad trained members of the NOI to avoid eating pork, which was considered unclean. Malcolm also stopped using foul language, which he had resorted to frequently when he was on the streets and also in prison. Another important tenet of Muhammad's religion, which Malcolm would get to know and embrace, was the unfortunate NOI idea that the white man was the devil in American society.[8]

MALCOLM X'S INITIAL MEETING WITH THE HONORABLE ELIJAH MUHAMMAD

The way Malcolm initially prepared himself to meet the Honorable Elijah Muhammad for the first time in future was admired by his two brothers, who were doing a lot already for the NOI as active members. They felt that the NOI leader was doing everything he could, through his responses to Malcolm's letters, to encourage the young prisoner to embrace the Islamic faith. With advice from his brothers to refrain from certain antisocial behaviors, Malcolm Little became a model prisoner. On August 7, 1952, he was paroled at a time when his letters to Muhammad had become very impressive and also filled with the faith of a true Islamic believer. It was on August 31, 1952, that Malcolm, accompanied by a delegation of about 200 Muslim NOI adherents, traveled to Chicago to hear a speech being given by Muhammad at Temple No. 2. NOI leaders of the group, including Malcolm's brothers, had alerted Muhammad to the fact that they were bringing their new convert called Malcolm Little who, after that day, would change his name to Malcolm X. As expected, Muhammad gave his speech, which met with thunderous applause. Behaving like a true prophet of his people, Muhammad leapt to his feet and called the name of Malcolm, exhorting him to come forward. In humility, Malcolm moved forward to receive much praise from Muhammad—something that also surprised the audience. The praise was for what Muhammad explained as Malcolm's gifted letter-writing ability. Muhammad also compared Malcolm's trials and tribulations to those of the Biblical Job, who likewise encountered many tribulations but never gave up. Muhammad held the belief that Malcolm was destined for greatness as well as leadership in the NOI and, above all, Muhammad felt unequivocally that, at all times, he could trust him, and that "Malcolm will be faithful."[9]

The NOI leaders present at the event were impressed by Malcolm's transparent humility. Some of them claimed that Malcolm stood so quiet and seemed so much bewildered by Muhammad's presence that he made it appear as if he, as a new Muslim convert, was encountering someone whose stature was similar to that of God. In his own written account later, Malcolm had confirmed that he could not open his mouth to say anything in Muhammad's presence. When he looked at

Elijah Muhammad, head of the Nation of Islam (NOI), is shown at a lectern in Chicago introducing Malcolm X on February 26, 1961. (AP Photo/Paul Cannon)

the Honorable Elijah Muhammad in veneration, he was completely awestruck, as he felt that the eyes of over 200 other Muslims were staring at him.[10] It was not surprising that Malcolm and the other new converts were attracted to the NOI because of the racial controversies during the time. They saw the NOI as a refuge against racial injustice. After Muhammad accepted Malcolm publicly into the NOI with unlimited praise, he welcomed Malcolm and other NOI members from Detroit to his mansion in Chicago for an arranged dinner.[11]

On that day, as part of his August 1952 conversion, Malcolm Little received the blessings of his NOI leaders to change his name to Malcolm X. For Malcolm, "Little" was a slave surname. At the dinner, the conversation centered on strategy, but not on the teachings of Islam. Malcolm silently vowed to follow the strategic instruction. He returned to Detroit to work very hard for the NOI. Elijah Muhammad heard about his dedication, and invited him back to Chicago and appointed him an assistant minister at Temple No. 1. There, Malcolm X preached impressive Islamic sermons. Muhammad, sensing Malcolm's continued faithfulness and resilience, decided to send him on national assignments to organize new temples and also to help revive older ones that were collapsing.[12]

Due to his transparent dedication as a Muslim leader-in-the-making, Malcolm was named a full-fledged minister of the NOI, and by the late 1950s, he became the chief spokesperson for the entire NOI organization nationwide. Also, of all of the NOI's appointed ministers, Malcolm was considered the group's most effective one. It was during this time that he was invited by the editors of the New York–based *Amsterdam News* newspaper to start writing a regular column about Islamic matters for publication in the newspaper. In fact, during this time, it also became useful for Muhammad, as the leader of the NOI, to agree to write a new column of his own in *Amsterdam News*. These arrangements were made by Malcolm X, who wanted to make sure that the NOI and its teachings would spread quickly. In June 1954, Malcolm was picked by Muhammad to go to New York to serve as the minister for Temple No. 7, with over one million black Muslim members.[13] In the new position, Malcolm appointed James 7X as his assistant minister, while another young NOI member called Joseph X served as the captain of the young, uniformed militant security wing of NOI known as Fruits of Islam (FOI).[14]

During this time, what Malcolm wanted to do as one of the young Islamic leaders was simply to show that he was a good Muslim, and that he was not in competition with his NOI leader, the Honorable Elijah Muhammad. Therefore, when Malcolm was informed that his request had been approved for Muhammad to write a weekly column for the Harlem-based newspaper, the *Amsterdam News*, he decided to switch his own arranged column to be published in another black newspaper in California known as the *Los Angeles Herald Dispatch*. He did not want it to seem that they were in competition. Through the columns that Malcolm wrote, he was very happily spreading news about his Muslim group in a national black newspaper. In the end, Malcolm felt that it would be better for the Muslims to have their own publication to serve as the NOI's mouthpiece and Islamic news outlet. In the fall of 1959, Malcolm sought permission from Muhammad and eventually established and registered a new periodical called the *Messenger Magazine*. Advertised widely in the *Amsterdam News* of Harlem, the publication was to propagate Muhammad's aims and accomplishments, as well as Islamic truths and successes. After a year of publication, the new magazine did not yield the desired readership and advertising support. Therefore, in 1960, Malcolm discontinued the periodical. Instead, he established the monthly newspaper that he named *Muhammad Speaks*, which reported on national and local news stories. Also, it published articles on various thematic issues, including health, education, and history, together with editorials on other topical issues. Throughout the country, as well as on college campuses and on the streets, young Muslim men were diligently selling copies of the newspaper in every major city in the United States.[15]

MALCOLM X'S HARD WORK WITH THE NATION OF ISLAM

Due to the hardworking efforts of Malcolm and other leaders, the NOI was growing by leaps and bounds. Its influence in the various black communities nationwide was growing as well. Furthermore, the membership of the group was growing steadily among African Americans within the United States' troubled cities, as residents were being attracted to its message and its programs.[16] At this time, Malcolm was traveling throughout the country as Elijah Muhammad's national spokesperson, often distributing copies of the NOI newspaper that carried news and other items about Muhammad and his organization. It was also the time that he made strenuous efforts to make contacts with Muslims overseas, especially those in the Middle East and Africa. They began to take a keen interest in the affairs of blacks in the United States. Furthermore, with Malcolm X and other young black leaders at the forefront of Islamic matters in the NOI, Muslims were now readily dealing with problems within various black communities—matters that white leaders were not addressing. Among these problems were drug use and addiction, which affected poor black neighborhoods. As part of a new six-point program, Malcolm's group treated drug addiction problems with seriousness. Seen as a plague in black communities that could no longer be tolerated, Malcolm X and other Muslim leaders saw it as a social as well as racial problem and also as an addiction that needed immediate assistance. In his autobiography, Malcolm explained that his group took steps similar to what was effectively used to treat alcohol addiction by the national organization called Alcoholics Anonymous.[17]

Many blacks saw the importance of Malcolm in the NOI, when they realized that the initiatives that he spearheaded—including the six-point program against drug addiction—were working successfully. The foregoing antidrug policy was put in place with the help of other NOI members, especially those who had gone through the program before. In fact, since Malcolm X tried to live an exemplary life of not smoking, drinking, and womanizing, as other Muslims did, he was able to attract many black adherents to the tenets of Islam. Even those who were drug addicts and considered doomed by society listened to Malcolm when he approached them with Islamic teachings and tried to woo them for the Islamic cause.

At the time, the tool that Malcolm X was able to use most effectively was his own dark past and tattered background. Malcolm was a tangible example of what it meant to be a lost person, in terms of religious and spiritual awareness, but could be redeemed if one had the faith and the determination to get help. The new converts also saw that there was hope for them, as they followed the teachings of Malcolm, who was known all over the country and even overseas as being a disciple of the Honorable Elijah Muhammad. In that capacity, Malcolm had to respect and accept the orders of his superior, the Honorable Elijah Muhammad. That, indeed, was why in 1957, he agreed to travel to Los Angeles, California, to establish one of the temples of the NOI. Malcolm chose to work from the office of the *Herald Dispatch* in the city, as he was interested in learning about how to organize a newspaper for publication. He used these skills to establish *Muhammad Speaks*, which was sold by NOI youngsters.

MALCOLM X'S MARRIAGE TO BETTY SANDERS IN 1958

As Malcolm X was being thrust onto the national public stage as a spokesman for the NOI, he had been thinking of the woman who would eventually become his wife and the future mother of his children. Ms. Betty Sanders had joined Temple No. 7 in Harlem, New York. A native of Detroit, Michigan, the young Ms. Sanders was born on May 28, 1934, and raised as a Catholic. She was a graduate of Tuskegee Institute (now Tuskegee University) in Alabama, where she had majored in education. In New York, she was seeking a professional degree in nursing as teaching jobs were limited at the time. Like Malcolm X, Betty Sanders had been raised in a home "where race issues played a prominent role."[18]

After becoming an active NOI member, Ms. Sanders took the name of Betty X and, soon after, she started to share her professional knowledge with the women and young ladies of the temple by giving lectures on personal hygiene. It was in her teaching capacity that Malcolm X initially became aware of Betty as he stopped by her class to keep tabs on what was being taught. Over time, he became impressed with her beauty, intelligence, and confidence, and he used the excuse of taking her to the Museum of Natural History for the purpose of getting information to share with Betty's new class. Also, Malcolm arranged for Betty to travel to Chicago, ostensibly for several days of training for new NOI teachers. Instead, he wanted Muhammad and his wife, Clara, to observe and report on her to Malcolm, and hence, she was a houseguest of the Muhammads. In the end, the NOI leader reported to Malcolm that Ms. Betty X "was a fine sister."[19]

Malcolm decided to propose to Betty. Therefore, on Sunday, January 12, 1958, Malcolm entered a Detroit telephone booth to propose to Betty, who accepted the proposal. [20] After that, Malcolm and Betty wanted to get married very fast and in a simple manner because both of them were busy. They did not have much time for elaborate arrangements for the marriage. Therefore, soon after the engagement in mid-January 1958, they drove to northern Indiana so that they could get married quickly across the Kentucky border. When that did not work out because of residency requirements for the marriage to take place, they came back to Detroit to obtain the required blood tests as well as to buy their rings. On February 14, 1958, Malcolm X and Betty X were married in East Lansing, Michigan, by the Justice of the Peace. Present as witnesses were Malcolm's brothers, Philbert and Reginald. Later, Elijah Muhammad informed members of the NOI of the marriage and most members celebrated the news. Malcolm's marriage to Betty was followed in less than one year by the birth of Atallah, the couple's first child. Atallah provided Malcolm with the sense of family that had eluded him as a child. While the marriage as well as the birth of his children provided roots, those roots did not hinder his wings of ascension as a rising star in the NOI. Betty described their marriage as "hectic, beautiful, and unforgettable—the greatest thing in my life."[21]

Malcolm's marriage to Betty was not without problems, as her foster parents were unhappy about it for various reasons. When Betty announced that she planned to marry Malcolm, her foster mother sobbed uncontrollably. She thought that Malcolm was too old for Betty as well as bemoaned the fact that he was not even a Christian. In contrast, the news of the marriage between Malcolm and Betty overjoyed Malcolm's siblings because they saw Betty as a stabilizing force in Malcolm's life. Between 1958 and 1960, Malcolm and Betty had three children, and they would have three more before he was murdered in 1967. Apart from Atallah Shabazz, the oldest, the other children of Malcolm and Betty—who were named after several prominent black leaders—were Qubilah Shabazz, Ilyasah Shabazz, Gamilah Lumumba Shabazz, Malikah Shabazz, and Malaak Shabazz. Eventually, Betty's foster parents started to enjoy her children as grandparents—a situation that helped in improving the relationship between them and Malcolm, their son-in-law.

Meanwhile, between 1961 and the time that Malcolm would finally leave the NOI to form his own organization in 1964, Malcolm X was concentrating his speeches on college campuses. There, he had receptive and enthusiastic audiences. They were, however, not without their controversies, as several university leaders feared that Malcolm, with his popularity among the black youth, would cause campus riots. That was why Malcolm's fall 1963 speech at the University of California at Berkeley was eventually cancelled by campus administrators. However, the organizers decided to have the event moved to the nearby Young Men's Christian Association (YMCA). At the time, Malcolm decided to widen his scope of audiences. In April 1961, he started to speak on Ivy League college campuses. At Yale, he agreed to debate Louis Lomax as well as planned an appearance on NBC Radio and Television network's "Open Mind" program. During the show, program host Eric Goldman introduced Malcolm as the number two man of the NOI, but Malcolm—for fear of a backlash from Muhammad—diplomatically denied that there was any such position in the NOI. The author James Baldwin was part of the panel, and the two men would afterward build a lifelong friendship up until Malcolm's death.[22]

Apart from powerful sermons and sermonettes that Malcolm preached in Islamic mosques and to black audiences in predominantly black churches, he also gave numerous powerful speeches. He visited such black churches as the African Methodist Episcopal (AME) Church, the Christian Methodist Episcopal Church, the Baptist Church, and others. Noteworthy speeches that Malcolm gave in the 1960s included the following: "The Ballot or the Bullet," "The Farce on Washington," "God's Judgment of White America," "Message to the Grassroots," and "There Is a Worldwide Revolution Going On," among others. "The Ballot or the Bullet" is considered one of the most important speeches that Malcolm X made in the 1960s during his Islamic militancy and fame because he used it to demonstrate the importance of his fellow blacks taking electoral events seriously. In fact, he also made it clear to his various audiences that both his sermons and speeches should be seen as an evangelical opportunity because, as he put it, the congregations that he addressed usually included first-time guests.[23]

MALCOLM X AND MARTIN LUTHER KING, JR.: DIFFERENT IN STYLE BUT WITH COMMON GOALS

Malcolm's growing prominence as a national speaker and Islamic leader inevitably led people to compare him with Dr. Martin Luther King, Jr. The admiration for one leader over another seemed to depend on the religious affiliation of black men and women who were comparing them. Also, it became clear to many blacks at this time that Malcolm X was one of their most vocal leaders, and that he, as a Muslim leader, and Dr. Martin Luther King, Jr., as a Christian minister and preacher, were fighting for the same cause—the civil rights of African Americans. They did so from different perspectives and from different podiums. Malcolm X was seen as a radical Islamic leader from Harlem, who meant well for his fellow blacks. Dr. King was seen by his Christian followers as the nonviolent and well-educated black preacher from the south, who embraced Gandhian principles of nonviolence, won a Nobel peace prize, and wanted to achieve civil as well as human rights for his fellow blacks during his lifetime. While Dr. King preached for civil rights and racial equality from Baptist Church pulpits, Malcolm used his Islamic sermons in temples and lectures on college campuses to address similar problems confronting the black race. At the time, other black leaders, including writers, were also contributing to what they saw as the common struggle for civil rights. For example, Manning Marable, in his 2011 book on Malcolm X, confirmed that racism was seen by Baldwin as well as by Dr. King, Malcolm, and indeed Dr. W. E. B. Du Bois, another leading black writer and scholar. The only difference was that, at the time, Malcolm and other NOI leaders were opposed to the integrationist goals of the march being planned by King and others to take place in 1963.[24]

These black leaders saw minorities suffering from racism as colored people, who were described by Marable as "Africans, Asians, Jews and other minorities."[25] In the context of racism, Marable further wrote that it was due to the abhorrence of racism by King, Baldwin, Malcolm, and Du Bois that these black leaders did not mince words but, instead, denounced the psychological way and social manner in which racism had been suffered by America's black population, especially in the Deep South. Unfortunately, several black men and women in the Christian churches saw these leaders differently. To them, Malcolm X, as a Muslim, and Baldwin, as an openly black homosexual, were unlike the middle-class and affluent civil rights leadership. That is why Marable quoted young blacks in the majority as seeing the two leaders as being the "polar opposite" of the Negro leadership of the widely known civil rights leadership, including Dr. King, Rev. Ralph David Abernathy, and others. They were not surprised that Dr. King had very little, in public, to do with Malcolm X. After all, they could not see how Christian ministers would fraternize easily with a staunch Muslim like Malcolm X as well as condone the openly gay behavior of Baldwin. Dr. King often preached that all men and women were God's children or creation.[26]

Although King and Malcolm X were differently raised—one in urban Georgia and the other in the northern black ghettos—they had

Martin Luther King and Malcolm X in their meeting at the U.S. Capitol on March 26, 1964. (Library of Congress)

much in common. The two religious leaders were alike in their quests for human dignity, as well as civil rights for their black brothers and sisters and other marginalized minorities or colored people. In American politics, Dr. King, at the time, was using his civil rights movement to encourage blacks to become politically aware, including urging them to register in large numbers to vote after the Voting Rights Act of 1964 was signed into law by President Lyndon B. Johnson. At the same time, Malcolm X was also using his sermons and lectures to encourage blacks to vote, including giving his memorable speech, "The Ballot or the Bullet." While King, in the 1960s, spoke eloquently from Baptist Church pulpits, Malcolm X expressed emotional outrage as his reaction to racial iniquities in urban and other contexts when he spoke on college campuses and at mosques as a guest speaker. According to Dr. Marable, the various phases of Malcolm X's life and growth initially showed him as an angry and bitter black man, who eventually became an icon that the black populace would revere and read about in separate publications written to analyze him as well as in his own 1967 co-authored autobiography. The deaths of Malcolm and Dr. King placed both of them in the annals of black heroes and martyrs. Both men were seen as iconic figures, and since their deaths, they have been equally honored in varied ways. Yet black poets and other writers, as Marable pointed out in his book about Malcolm, regarded the Muslim leader as their fallen idol.[27]

During this period, the Honorable Elijah Muhammad had moved from Chicago to Phoenix, Arizona, where he was running his NOI. In April 1963, Malcolm flew to Phoenix to meet Muhammad, whose wife, Clara, had threatened to leave him because of infidelity and rumors of fathering children out of wedlock. Upon the arrival of Malcolm in their Phoenix home, he was warmly welcomed, but instead of talking in the sitting room, as was customary, Muhammad led him through the inner doors to the swimming pool area, where they could talk freely. Malcolm boldly went to Arizona to confront Muhammad regarding stories circulating about his personal life, including womanizing. Malcolm felt that the image of his mentor as well as the NOI was at stake, and he was willing to do whatever he could in Muhammad's defense. For example, Malcolm and other NOI leaders back in New York and other places agreed that they would be able to couch the infidelities in prophetic terms, including the fact that David and several biblical leaders fell from grace because of womanizing, some of them even being accused of taking the wives of other men. Upon his return to the East Coast from Arizona, Malcolm X thought about various ways to cover up his mentor's many extramarital affairs and the birth of several children out of wedlock. Over time, however, he became uncomfortable with the situation. His efforts to shield the transgressions of the NOI leader were creating enemies for Malcolm within the ranks of some Chicago-based leaders, who were already disgusted with what they perceived as Muhammad's anti-Muslim behavior. Some important NOI leaders, who did not condone Muhammad's behavior, reportedly began to build the ground work for the eventual downfall of both Malcolm X and Muhammad.[28]

HOW THE PUBLIC AND MALCOLM X SAW MUHAMMAD'S MANY WOMEN

Interestingly, black Muslim leaders began to give the impression that since Muslims, under polygamous arrangements, could have up to four wives at one time, the Honorable Elijah Muhammad could make a similar claim. The difference, as Malcolm X and other NOI leaders began to see, was that the Koran, the Islamic holy book, expected a Muslim with many wives to do so openly and also treat the wives equally. However, as Malcolm X and others realized, Muhammad did not live openly with the women and, also, when confronted, he did not confirm paternity for the many children that the women reportedly bore for him. To try to make some of the women seem like liars, the NOI leader reportedly encouraged one of his assistants by the name of Isaiah Karriem to describe two of the said women in *Muhammad Speaks*, the NOI editorial mouthpiece, as prostitutes. After all, the public knew Clara Muhammad as Muhammad's only wife and, therefore, his future surviving widow.[29]

It seemed as if the Muslim and Christian black leaders of the time had much in common, irrespective of their religious faith or affiliation. Dr. King, for example, had been accused of unproven marital infidelities in the 1960s, and the NOI leader, Muhammad, was similarly accused of infidelities. Other close associates of Muhammad too became targets of FBI investigations. As Marable confirmed, the FBI was very much aware of Muhammad's infidelities, "thanks to its wiretaps and informants."[30] What was remarkable about Malcolm X was that, as a public figure, he lived a clean life. It was free from drugs and womanizing, unlike many other religious and even civil rights leaders. That was why the FBI, according to Marable's biography, was frustrated as it failed in its attempts "to find Malcolm's weaknesses."[31]

To make matters worse for Muhammad, the FBI reportedly approved the text of a letter detailing Muhammad's infidelities to be sent to his wife as well as to Malcolm and the other NOI leaders. The Bureau did this as a way of sowing a seed of confusion and dissension in the ranks of the NOI. What surprised and disappointed Malcolm was that Muhammad, as his mentor, had preached against extramarital affairs. Yet, as it turned out, he could not control his own sexual appetite. In fact, Malcolm and others knew that in order for Muhammad to keep his affairs under wraps and to make them a private issue between himself and his mistresses, he reportedly rented in Chicago "love-nest" apartments away from his regular place of abode. Unfortunately, the FBI knew about these Muhammad hideouts. FBI director J. Edgar Hoover gave approval so that agents could install "telephone taps and electronic bugging devices in the apartments."[32]

Malcolm X was very careful not to say anything publicly or otherwise about the happenings in Muhammad's household. It was important for him to continue to show allegiance and respect for his NOI spiritual leader. Like several other NOI members, Malcolm eventually became disenchanted with the stories about Muhammad's infidelities. He was able to deal with the situation because, as it had become apparent, Malcolm did hear much earlier the rumors about Muhammad, but he refused to examine as to whether they were true or not. It was mainly because he was known to dislike people, even scholars, who accused others by basing their facts on limited sources. For example, between 1961 and 1962, Malcolm had the chance to listen to several speakers, including those who attacked Muslims. One of them was Harvard University History professor Arthur Schlesinger, Jr., who served as a special assistant to President John F. Kennedy. The Pulitzer Prize–winner gave a 1962 talk at Atlanta University and, since Malcolm was in town, he attended the hour-long lecture, titled "America's Domestic

Future, Its Perils and Prospects." Since Schlesinger was not allied with any religious group, he gave his lecture as an intellectual exercise, and his audience appreciated it very much, as he helped his listeners to be able to use the facts to judge Malcolm and other black leaders that the speaker commented on. For example, during the lecture, Professor Schlesinger instead praised such black leaders as the former Supreme Court justice Thurgood Marshall, at the time an NAACP attorney who would later become Solicitor-General in the Kennedy administration. He also praised Roy Wilkins and the late Rev. Dr. Martin Luther King, Jr. Most of Schlesinger's praise was based on the fact that these black leaders advanced effective ways to achieve equality either through the courts or peacefully. Quoting from an article by William Worthy, a black journalist, Schlesinger agreed that black Muslims were racists. Malcolm did not accept that depiction and, instead, he questioned how and why a Harvard historian would base his conclusions on one source (Worthy's article) to indict the entire Muslim population that way. When Malcolm X queried him, Professor Schlesinger wanted to show that Malcolm X was either ignorant or did not know what he was talking about, as he asked if he had read the Worthy article. Malcolm showed that he had read the article and also disputed Schlesinger's claim that it described black Muslims as being racists. Instead, Malcolm pointed out that what Worthy meant was how the very conditions, which led to the creation of the NOI, were of racist and even oppressive nature.[33]

MALCOLM X AND THE HONORABLE ELIJAH MUHAMMAD IN THE 1960s

During this period of the early 1960s, Malcolm X was becoming disillusioned about the corruption he was hearing about in the NOI. Yet he still listened and tried to learn from his mentor, the Honorable Elijah Muhammad. Malcolm utilized every opportunity to promote Muhammad's thoughts in order to show a difference between the second phase of the U.S. civil rights movement that Dr. King was leading and their own NOI. To the surprise of many, Muhammad, in the spring of 1963, did openly level criticisms against Dr. King's movement after demonstrations in Birmingham, in which King sought integration for blacks and whites. Muhammad described Dr. King as being a fool in an interview that appeared in the April 30, 1963, edition of the *New York Herald Tribune*, citing his opposition to Dr. King's integrationist appeals. Astonishingly, Muhammad compared the black civil rights leader to a dog that waddled around a door with a hope of "gaining the favor of its master."[34]

During this period, Malcolm X started to speak angrily about civil and human rights issues. Like Elijah Muhammad, Malcolm grew disgusted that Dr. King and his followers upheld the Gandhian notion of passive resistance and nonviolence, in spite of the abuse that local law enforcement officials and their police dogs had visited on the black demonstrators. Muhammad felt angry to the point that he said publicly that if Dr. King and his civil rights demonstrators had responded with violence and, as a result, also attacked the white law enforcement officials and their dogs, that could have been seen as a justification by "God and the Divine law of self-defense."[35]

Between 1964 and 1965, a black leader whose violent rhetoric was praised repeatedly by Muhammad was Harlem U.S. Congressman Adam Clayton Powell, Jr. Muhammad felt that Powell's criticism of what he considered to be antiblack and middle class was part of the prevailing politics of the Republican Party. Powell, who would later lose his U.S. congressional seat to the younger politician, Charles Rangel, felt that he and his fellow radical black leaders might be able to achieve the needed progress in their lives. For the first time, Muhammad, who did not like to offer an open endorsement of political figures, also agreed that progress could, as well, be attained through what he saw as a judicious use of the ballot box. At the time, Powell was seen as a possible national leader and an alternative to Dr. King and others in national black leadership. Hoover, the FBI leader, became tired of Muhammad's attacks on white political leaders while he praised Powell and others. Therefore, the Bureau leaked information on Muhammad's prison sentence, jail term, and his past criminal record. That was considered a bombshell because Muhammad had succeeded in shielding the fact that, under his former name of Elijah Poole, he had actually gone to jail in Georgia. As further shown, the FBI, as a federal security and intelligence agency, had amassed what history professor Claude Andrew Clegg III of Indiana University described in his much-praised biography of Muhammad, *An Original Man: The Life and Times of Elijah Muhammad,* as a considerable amount of information. This included details about Muhammad's movements as well as very sensitive information to embarrass several NOI top officials. As confirmed in Professor Clegg's book, what the FBI leaders and their agents were bent on leaking to the American public were neither lies nor exaggerated information. Instead, they were what existed as facts in the criminal record file of Elijah Poole, the former name that Muhammad was known by.[36]

Muhammad tried to find ways of diffusing the impact of Hoover's plans to embarrass him and other NOI leaders. In fact, in a response that Muhammad would encourage to be published in an August 1963 issue of *Muhammad Speaks,* an editorial content indirectly challenged claims and materials that the FBI leaked to the Los Angeles–based *Herald Examiner.* Apart from merely denying that he, Muhammad, and his supporters were not liars in denying the FBI claims, the NOI leader was still waiting for a national opportunity to speak out against the actions of Hoover and his FBI.[37] Indeed, Muhammad sought a fine opportunity to speak to a large Muslim audience in order to defend himself. His chance came in the fall of 1963. It was on October 13, 1963, when he had the opportunity to speak at Flint, Michigan, to more than 4,000 NOI faithful believers, including Malcolm X. Muhammad was still being watched because the city attorney, Edward Joseph, had sent a large number of local law enforcement officials to make sure that the lecture would not become violent. That was in spite of the fact that Muhammad had his own security from the FOI, the uniformed young Muslims who served as security officers at functions. The presence of the white police officers often caused tension, and as a result, Malcolm X and other NOI leaders agreed that Muhammad should end the event halfway. That was when Muhammad vowed that he would never again allow white officers, whether armed or not, to come into a place where he was speaking. Malcolm X watched the events keenly, especially since there were rumors at the time that Muhammad's health was not in good shape. For his quietness and obedience to Muhammad, there were also rumors—some allegedly generated by the FBI—that "Malcolm X was making a pile of money."[38]

In reality, Malcolm and his family had very little money. That is why Betty often encouraged Malcolm to save money for their future needs. These discussions became intense, especially as their children increased in number and they also started to go to school, with needs of their own. Instead of agreeing to do as Betty wished, including thinking about financial savings for the future of the family, Malcolm made his wife understand that if anything were to happen to him as a leader of the NOI, the organization would take care of her for life, as a widow, as well as their children until they were grownups. Later, Malcolm recounted that "I could never have been a bigger fool."[39]

Later on, Malcolm discovered that he was completely wrong about what the NOI would do for his family if he were to die in the midst of his Islamic work. In fact, he was so dedicated to his mentor that he revealed later in life that whenever he spoke, as NOI spokesperson, he made sure of saying that he represented the Honorable Elijah Muhammad. He consistently encouraged members of his audiences, who wished to have the real truth, to travel to Chicago to meet Muhammad. That is because Malcolm deferred to the NOI leader as the real messenger of God (or Allah, as Muslims call God). Also, Malcolm made it clear to his friends and Muslim associates that his briefcase was stocked not with heaps of cash, but only with photographs of the NOI leader, so that whenever his photo was snapped by reporters, he pleaded with them, instead, to use Muhammad's photo in the publication. He did so because he did not want to do anything to offend the Honorable Elijah Muhammad. Malcolm X also made it plain that irrespective of his national and international importance, he still owed complete loyalty to the NOI leader, adding that he would still follow Muhammad "as faithful and as selfless a servant to him [Muhammad] as I was."[40]

Malcolm painfully realized that Betty's anguish about their family's lack of resources was well placed. It was becoming more and more apparent that the NOI would not be there for his family if anything were to happen to him. Therefore, he modified certain things he did for the organization and for some of its members. He also became hypersensitive to the criticisms that he was getting from other NOI leaders because of jealousy. Some of the unflattering comments emanated from the fact that his photographs and interviews were often in the American news media. Due to his agreement with Betty that their family should start saving some funds for their future needs, or the proverbial

rainy day, Malcolm immediately stopped using his own money to sponsor the trips of other NOI members from his New York mosque to
travel elsewhere simply to "lay groundwork for new mosques in other
cities."[41] Before that, he did not realize that spending his own funds to
pay for expensive NOI activities, including advertisements that made
Muhammad look good, did reinforce Betty's worries about money. Initially, there was no indication that Malcolm would adhere to his wife's
suggestion or wishes for him to curtail out-of-pocket expenses for NOI
activities. However, he started to modify his activities, and especially
to try to reduce the expensive publicity in which his name appeared as
the financial sponsor, including newspaper and other media advertising
for the NOI paid for with his own funds. What was remarkable about
Malcolm, however, was that several publications, including *Life Magazine* and *Newsweek Magazine*, wanted to do interviews with or about
him. However, he declined invitations of such nature, although some
of the interviews could have earned him much-needed money. He did
so because he did not want things to seem as if he was competing with
his mentor, Muhammad. Yet, in the end, he was sad about refusing to
be the focus of these would-be publicity activities, especially as he felt
that each of the refusals he made "was a general loss for the black man
and for the Nation of Islam."[42]

Undoubtedly, Malcolm X knew the value of publicity. As a result, he was sad to turn down press appearances in order to reduce or
minimize jealousy emanating from his fellow NOI leaders, including
Muhammad himself. For example, he had the opportunity to appear on
the television program *Face the Nation*, but declined the invitation.
Apart from the general jealousy that he felt from or among his colleagues in NOI, he was also not happy with the general attitude of the
Chicago headquarters of the NOI. He seemed to be in anguish about
the self-imposed restrictions or silence that he had placed on himself.
For example, Malcolm felt that it was very much unlike him either to
remain silent or to make lukewarm statements about important events
affecting fellow blacks. In Malcolm's public lectures at this time, he
gave as examples the assassination in 1963 of Medgar Evers, the Mississippi Field Secretary of the National Association for the Advancement
of Colored people (NAACP) as well as when a bomb was exploded
in the black Christian church in Birmingham that killed four young

black girls in Sunday school. Malcolm did make statements, but as he tried to explain, they were not exactly the lukewarm words that he really wished to have been said about the bad climate of hate. In his opinion, "the American white man was generating and nourishing hatred."[43]

THE SADNESS OF MALCOLM X DESPITE SUCCESSES IN NOI

Malcolm X seemed confused and sad at the same time about his plight in the NOI. He could not understand how Muhammad would publicly praise him, but as he learned later, would privately undermine Malcolm X. He started to ponder over several examples. As he confirmed in his autobiography, the Honorable Elijah Muhammad had gone to the extent of singling him out to be made the first National Minister of NOI. Also, very unusually, at a 1963 Philadelphia NOI rally, Muhammad publicly invited him to the podium for him to be embraced by his mentor, a sign of both affection and importance in the organization. Furthermore, in Muhammad's own words, Malcolm was his most faithful and hardworking minister around. He said that he also trusted the young national leader, adding about Malcolm that "He will follow me until he dies."[44]

Malcolm X had heard about a Ku Klux Klan (KKK) reward for his death. Yet, he felt that he faced much more imminent danger from within the NOI circles. At the time, Malcolm had been a minister of the NOI for 12 years, and he was beginning to feel the heat about being a Muslim. During that time in 1963, Malcolm X wrote that he started to speak less of religion, but instead more of "social doctrine to Muslims, and current events, and politics."[45]

By late 1963, Malcolm started to be sensible, as he decided to try and end his antiwhite rhetoric. For example, he recalled that several words he had uttered and quoted in the national press ruffled several Islamic and non-Islamic feathers. An example was in 1962, when a plane crash on June 3 of that year killed 121 travelers, including several leading American citizens. Malcolm described the tragedy as a very beautiful thing, further praying that other planes full of white passengers should fall out of the American sky because, as he said to the satisfaction of Muhammad and other NOI leaders, God was displeased with white Americans. The public was horrified by Malcolm's words about the crash, yet the Honorable Elijah Muhammad did not deem it necessary to impose any sanction on his minister. That is because several people in NOI circles felt he knew too much about the ugly and immoral aspects of Muhammad's life. Yet that was not so but instead, it seemed that Malcolm had not touched on a real sensitive matter of public interest. For example, when President John F. Kennedy was assassinated on Friday, November 22, 1963, in Dallas, all Americans, including Muslims, were shocked. In spite of Muhammad's public and private opinions on white Americans, for various reasons, he had an admiration for Kennedy and his Democratic Party administration.[46]

Attorney-General Robert F. Kennedy, a brother of President Kennedy, was seen by Malcolm and other NOI leaders as the supervisor of the FBI and its leadership at the same time that the FBI was interfering with Muhammad and his NOI. Therefore, President Kennedy's death could be used as an occasion for the NOI to show its pleasure at the assassination. Instead, to be on the safe side, Muhammad urged his followers, including Malcolm X, not to say anything publicly or quotable about the assassination of the U.S. president. In fact, apart from expressing shock about the death, he also made it known that he saw nothing useful to his NOI and its members emanating out of the killing. Therefore, when he was billed, on December 1, 1963, to speak to an NOI audience of about 700 in New York, he sent Malcolm to do so for him. The tempting topic was "God's Judgment on White America." The speech went well until during the question and answer part, when Malcolm was asked about the death of President Kennedy barely nine days previously (on November 22). Although Malcolm knew that Elijah Muhammad had an embargo on any NOI member making any statement about President Kennedy's death, he decided to answer the question. Yet, the available records point to the fact that Malcolm did say that the assassinated president simply became a victim of the foul and violent status quo. Malcolm felt that Kennedy had become a victim of the very violence that his administration had tolerated in other places, including Vietnam, the Congo (in Africa), Alabama, and in America's Deep South. The reporters further noted that Malcolm then added that he was such an old farm boy that "chickens coming home to roost never did make me sad, they have always made me glad."[47]

According to reports on Malcolm's statements at the New York event, the remarks about the Kennedy assassination were interpreted in various ways. At the same time, to a few other people, Malcolm's statements simply underscored the essence of events in their own NOI, including the rivalry that they suspected within their own ranks. Not remaining silent about the assassination, as Muhammad had directed, made several observers within and outside the NOI feel that Malcolm was either being defiant or trying to challenge Muhammad, who saw himself as the supreme Messenger of God (Allah). At this time, Muhammad and others pieced together the unexpected horrible comments he made about the assassination as well as the undiplomatic words or language he used when the plane crash had killed 121 travelers from Georgia. Consequently, Muhammad summoned Malcolm X to attend a December 2, 1963, meeting at the Chicago headquarters of the NOI. It could be seen that it was a tense meeting between the two top leaders of NOI. Malcolm's public statements about the Kennedy assassination were seen by Muhammad as being very much ill-timed; Muhammad also made it clear to Malcolm that the fact that those ill-timed words came from Malcolm, as a spokesperson for NOI, did have a bad reflection on all Muslims. In order for all Muslims to be disassociated from Malcolm X's horrible words, the Honorable Elijah Muhammad, to the surprise of many NOI members, said unequivocally that he would "have to silence him for the next ninety days."[48]

Malcolm X, who had over the years been Muhammad's disciple and rising star at the same time, did not object to the 90-day sanction. Instead, he said he agreed with him completely. What surprised Malcolm and his admirers was that soon after the meeting, national officials of NOI were instructed to spread the news about the punishment meted out to Malcolm. Therefore, these NOI leaders sent several messages, including telegrams, to various news organizations. Furthermore, they also used comments and articles in their own mouthpiece, *Muhammad Speaks* newspaper, to show their staunch loyalty to Muhammad at that time and, in effect, did very much to distance themselves from Malcolm X. What was sad was that the NOI headquarters wanted to make sure that Malcolm was totally demoted and disgraced. Therefore, they took steps to enhance the authority of Malcolm X's second-in-command at Mosque No. 7, Captain Joseph X. Muhammad's sanction included that Malcolm X would, for the 90 days, not say anything on behalf of the NOI or in public. The FBI knew everything that was going on through its agents within the NOI as well as from wiretaps, as Muhammad's phone conversations were being tapped. What would make Malcolm X decide to leave the NOI in the future was the fact that Muhammad, his mentor for many years, became antagonistic after the sanctioning of the prominent minister, and it was clear that Muhammad did it because of his own insecurity.[49]

In the eyes of many observers within and also outside the NOI, it was sad that the Honorable Elijah Muhammad, who had built up Malcolm X and promoted him through the ranks of his NOI, eventually turned around to undermine him. After all, it was very clear that Malcolm thought that he was acting in concert with the interest of Muhammad in mind, including castigating white people that the NOI leader often referred to as being devils. Of course, the FBI and its head, J. Edgar Hoover, were among those happy that such a discord had emerged between Muhammad his national spokesman and minister, Malcolm X. It was the beginning of the end of the father–son relationship that Muhammad and Malcolm had shared and from which the NOI had benefitted.

Chapter 3

THE SPLIT WITH
THE NATION OF ISLAM

The rift that had been growing between Malcolm X and other leaders of the Nation of Islam (NOI) deepened. Initially, the entire problem began as acts of jealousy expressed by other ministers, who spread the rumor that Malcolm was attracting too much attention, that he was not deferring enough of the spotlight to Muhammad as the NOI leader, and that he had NOI top leadership ambitions as well. Unfortunately for Malcolm, there were also hard feelings against him from Muhammad's children and grandchildren, who thought that Malcolm had taken their rightful place as Muhammad's most trusted confidant in the organization.

Malcolm, at the time, was one of the young NOI leaders who opposed Muhammad's order for NOI members not to have partisan political involvement, especially at the time of heightened political activity during political party primaries as well as during political protests, mass marches, and demonstrations by other American citizens. Muhammad, who was known to support Harlem's U.S. representative Adam Clayton Powell, Jr., thought that it was useless to participate in a political system that, in his opinion, was either doomed to failure or bound to fail in the end. He also feared that any open NOI activity opposing elected officials could bring down the wrath of the government on his organization and open past wounds, including the fact that Muhammad refused to serve in the U.S. Army on religious grounds and had encouraged Muhammad Ali, the heavyweight boxer, to do the same. At age of 22, Ali, born Cassius M. Clay, Jr., on January 17, 1942, beat fellow American boxer Sonny Liston to become the world's heavyweight boxing champion. The same year, in 1964, he became a member of the NOI, and hence he refused to be enlisted in the U.S. Army to fight in Vietnam on Islamic religious grounds. Apart from his respect for Muhammad as NOI leader, he was also a close friend of Malcolm X, who was supposed to have influenced him to become a Muslim and, in the process, to change his name to Muhammad Ali. As the NOI leader, Muhammad utilized the opportunity to make a public pronouncement about Ali's conversion by claiming publicly that he was very glad that "Cassius Clay admits he's a Muslim."[1]

Malcolm felt that Muhammad, as the NOI leader, was being hypocritical. After all, he knew about the NOI leader's staunch financial and material support for Clayton, the Harlem congressman. Yet, when Malcolm dared to protest against the public political stance of Muhammad, including the NOI leader's claim of being against NOI members getting involved in partisan political activity, Muhammad privately and publicly insisted on an apology, which Malcolm tendered but felt humiliated about doing so. However, such Muhammad-demanded apologies did not prevent Malcolm's subsequent support for political actions that, in his opinion, aimed at fighting or undermining black racial oppression; he sometimes did so very subtly.[2]

Furthermore, an impassable breach between Malcolm X and Muhammad was a difference in their respective moral standards as well. While Malcolm X tried his best to adhere to the Islamic religious doctrine about moral purity and marital fidelity of the NOI, Muhammad, as the leader, thought otherwise. In fact, Muhammad was known to have been involved in several extramarital relationships that had reportedly caused him to father at least a dozen children with other women. Malcolm saw that behavior as being hypocritical, as he felt that it was unacceptable that Muhammad severely disciplined NOI members who engaged in similar immoral behavior—either through extramarital affairs or simply by having children out of wedlock—including a woman who was known to have had a child for him in California. It was very troubling for Malcolm that, for several years, he had been aware of Muhammad's immoral conduct as well as his out-of-wedlock children, but he could not do anything about it if he chose to remain as an active NOI member. At best, what Malcolm X could do, under the prevailing unfortunate circumstances, was to make his displeasure about Muhammad be known to other like-minded NOI leaders, who would listen to him and help him find a solution.[3]

Muhammad heard that Malcolm had started to talk about his immoral behavior. Therefore, to counteract the danger that Malcolm could cause to his NOI leadership and prestige, Muhammad planned to act decisively. That was why, in the summer of 1964, Muhammad used his annual "Savior's Day" speech to a large gathering of NOI members and invited guests—an occasion that also celebrated the founding of the NOI—to take a swipe at Malcolm through a public ridicule of his known mentee. Without mentioning Malcolm by name, Muhammad claimed that an individual in the NOI wanted to be like him, in terms of wealth and leadership stature. He added that the person could not be what he, as NOI leader, happened to be because, as Muhammad told the large audience, the said subordinate NOI member who was trying to usurp his position as NOI leader at the time had not received divine revelations that he—Muhammad—received from Allah (God) to make him be acceptable to the NOI membership as leader, thus making it impossible for anyone—including Malcolm X—to challenge Muhammad's NOI leadership in any manner.[4]

Several supporters of Malcolm X in the NOI knew the context and also saw what Muhammad was doing to undermine his credibility as the NOI national minister and spokesperson. Unhappy with Muhammad and his cronies, Malcolm's supporters took it upon themselves to reveal a lot more to the public and also to Malcolm about Muhammad's moral decadence, including the specific fact that he had secret extramarital relationships with NOI's female secretaries. They further alleged that some of the secretaries also had children by Muhammad. To make matters worse, these supporters also revealed to Malcolm that Muhammad had extramarital affairs with white women, although he was still teaching his NOI followers to consider all white men and women as devils. Finally, Malcolm could no longer deny the truth about the dark side of NOI affairs. This was especially so because Malcolm was with Muhammad in an NOI office when two of Muhammad's former secretaries paid the NOI leader a surprise visit holding the babies they had borne him. Such matters had prompted over a dozen NOI members to defect to other organizations, and some worried NOI members who decided to stay in the organization with Malcolm asked Malcolm to confront Muhammad about these unfortunate matters.[5]

With the "cat out of the bag" about Muhammad's immoral conduct, Malcolm could no longer close his eyes to the truth that his hero and NOI mentor was, indeed, morally corrupt. He was also troubled that the leader that he had basically worshipped as well as respected unconditionally was guilty of the immoral lapses of which Malcolm had been made aware. Malcolm saw the hypocritical side of Muhammad at that time, especially as the NOI leader apparently engaged in the very behavior for which he condemned others. Malcolm was left with the painful truth that although the religious doctrine of the NOI strictly forbade extramarital affairs, the leader of the organization was not only involved in them, but he had also shown unrepentant behavior. What further surprised Malcolm was that Mrs. Clara Muhammad was silent about her husband's extramarital affairs, although she was supposed to have known "about the extramarital activities of her husband [Muhammad] as early as January 1960."[6]

Equally important for Malcolm was the existing understanding that all NOI members were expected to live by the moral and leadership examples of Muhammad as their leader. It was also supposed that an example of moral uprightness on the part of the NOI leader could be a way of keeping all of them within the bounds of moral purity as NOI rank and file. Therefore, if it became known to NOI converts and outsiders that Muhammad, as their leader, was morally impure, then the NOI's future could either be bleak or have disastrous consequences. Malcolm further felt that if the truth about Muhammad's immoral behavior was revealed, it would easily lead to the end of his own active participation in the NOI—an organization that he considered to be an important religious movement that represented his life's work. At that point, Malcolm was, in the eyes of the American public, one of the key national leaders of the NOI; hence he did not want the organization's image or leadership tarnished. Yet, Muhammad's extramarital affairs with black women, in particular, were contradicting several of his stated religious and moral beliefs, especially as Malcolm had re-echoed Muhammad's teaching to NOI rank and file that black women were to be respected, but not misused or violated. The reason for the respect of black women in that way, Muhammad had explained, was that these women were both the mothers of civilization through whom nations have been built, adding in Muhammad's teaching that, in particular, black women should be considered as extremely important as "the nurturers and first teachers of the children, who will eventually inherit the movement [NOI]."[7]

MALCOLM LEAVES THE NOI

Malcolm, at the time, started to have inner turmoil, yet he felt compelled to remain a few more months in the NOI to see if things would change. Also, having invested considerable effort in the organization, he was prepared to overlook some of the increasing hostility directed toward him by Muhammad and his NOI cronies, as well as hoped that the moral decadence of Muhammad would soon end. Instead of leaving the NOI in bitterness or anger, Malcolm entertained the hope of having an eventual reconciliation with Muhammad. At one point, Malcolm thought that he could use his friendship with Muhammad Ali, the heavyweight boxing champion, to return to his former NOI prominence or at least to return to Temple Number 7. However, he realized that for various reasons that would not be so. For example, during Muhammad's "Savior's Day" celebration in 1964, he overlooked Malcolm and, instead, invited Ali to the podium to shower glowing praises on the boxer. Apart from that, Malcolm heard from various sources about Ali's frequent trips to Chicago to meet Muhammad and, indeed, to play with his grandchildren, some of whom were of Ali's age at the time. Malcolm, who saw Ali as his close friend from the time the boxing legend joined the NOI in 1964, was dismayed and, as a result, felt that the best way left for him to keep his dignity was to leave the NOI completely.[8]

Eventually, however, it became clear to Malcolm that Muhammad had no intention of restoring him to his previous leadership roles, and that a pro-Muhammad NOI leadership faction was allegedly instigating plots to have Malcolm hurt in any way possible. Furthermore, Malcolm had suffered unlimited indignities for several months. At that point, Malcolm contemplated adopting several measures, but he realized that he was actually left with only two viable options, instead of making the difficult decision to move on. The options were that either Malcolm could fully capitulate in order to forget the past, or he could secede from the NOI with his followers, which would mean forming his own splinter Islamic group. He did not follow either of the two options. Instead, on March 8, 1964, Malcolm held a press conference to announce his formal departure from the NOI and the creation of his new organization known as the Muslim Mosque, Incorporated (MMI). Eight days later, on March 16, the MMI became a legal entity, as Malcolm went to file a certificate of incorporation with the county of New York. The Hotel Theresa was its legal headquarters.[9]

What did surprise many people in and outside of the NOI was that Malcolm made it plain that he was leaving the NOI, but that other members of the organization—including many of them that he recruited—should still remain in it with his blessings; at the time, the NOI had over one million members nationally. Yet, Malcolm encouraged the NOI converts that he had recruited to remain under the continuing spiritual leadership of Muhammad. Also, very surprisingly, Malcolm told members of the NOI that he would be able to spread Muhammad's message in the best possible way by operating outside his Islamic organization. Malcolm's plan was to work hard among the other millions of non-Muslim blacks in the United States to get many of them to join his new organization, adding: "I remain a Muslim."[10]

According to Malcolm and his supporters, he took the steps on March 8, 1964, to move out of the religious domination and shadow of Muhammad and his NOI organization. Consequently, Malcolm worked very hard to soften some of the militant and hard-edged public pronouncements that he had made in the past as an NOI national leader. He worked hard on other issues, especially with respect to race in general, and whites in particular. Malcolm did his best to distance himself from the NOI philosophy that all white people were devils—indeed by saying, among other things, that he still felt there were sincere white men and women in the United States. As part of what Malcolm saw as his process of atonement, he also stated that he was going on a holy pilgrimage to Mecca and, later, to Africa (which he referred to as the motherland) in search of spiritual renewal. An important reason for his trip to Mecca, as he explained to a thunderous applause in a meeting with his supporters, was that it would allow him to make himself into an authentic Muslim, considering himself not to be either a mainstream or an authentic Muslim at the time. Several of those giving Malcolm the thunderous applause were new recruits of his organization and also non-Muslims who liked to listen to his lectures, as he kept his word not to attract any NOI members into his new organization, unless they left on their own volition and joined the MMI—as some of them did.[11]

Apart from establishing the MMI to continue his Islamic interests, Malcolm also made it clear during his March 8 press conference that part of his plans was to establish a black nationalist political organization to engage in nonpartisan political activism. Furthermore, he also had plans to align himself, as a black man, with some of the existing civil rights organizations, including groups such as the Student Nonviolent Coordinating Committee (SNCC), led by Stokely Carmichael (who later changed his own name to Kwame Ture to honor Ghana's president Kwame Nkrumah and Guinea's president Sekou Toure), and Congress of Racial Equality (CORE), led by James Farmer.[12]

Unfortunately, his former colleagues in the NOI felt that none of the new programs Malcolm announced was in tune with Muhammad's NOI, thus confirming that Malcolm's break from the NOI had personal and ideological implications. Although Malcolm did not directly or publicly blame Muhammad for his departure from the NOI, he still did accuse some of his NOI national leadership colleagues based in Chicago as being in cahoots or conspiracy with his critics for him to leave the black Muslim organization, especially if he were to retain his peace of mind. Malcolm, in trying not to be ungrateful to Muhammad, did go on to point out that one of the best ways to confront America's racial strife was to follow Muhammad's teachings on disintegration of the races—a public statement that surprised several of Malcolm's admirers, especially as Malcolm had promised to distance himself from some of his past violent rhetoric.[13]

MALCOLM X'S CONVERSION TO SUNNI ISLAM

Malcolm's move to establish his own Muslim organization created a desire in him to learn more about the historic origins of Islam and the black race. That is why he embarked on active plans to take trips to Mecca on a pilgrimage as well as subsequently visit the continent of Africa. In order to make the planned Islamic and African journeys successful, Malcolm needed money to purchase his airline ticket as well as to file the requisite tourist visa applications, which would allow him to enter the Islamic holy land and the African countries. He also knew that, as a rule, only *bona fide* Muslims would be allowed to join worldwide Muslims to perform the annual pilgrimage that was known as the *hajj*. Consequently, Malcolm began to cultivate ties with the Federation of Islamic Associations in the United States and Canada so that he could get the needed documents and a letter of introduction to support his application for a visa, and also, to introduce him to immigration officials in the Kingdom of Saudi Arabia. Eventually, Malcolm obtained the money that he needed for the ticket from his half-sister Ella, with a promise to pay her back. He also worked hard to secure the proper documentation from the federation for a successful application to obtain the requisite visa as well as a letter of introduction that would establish his credentials as a bona fide Muslim. Furthermore, he also cultivated friendships with African diplomats at the United Nations, thus making it a lot easier to get a visa for the African trip. On April 13, 1964, Malcolm X departed for the Middle East. He arrived first in Cairo, Egypt, for a brief sightseeing trip as well as to attend part of the year's meeting of the Organization of African Unity (OAU), a conclave of elected African leaders, which enabled Malcolm to meet several leaders from independent African nations; he had planned the trip that way to be able to attend the OAU meeting before paying visits to several independent African countries after his Islamic pilgrimage in Mecca.[14]

After visiting Cairo, Malcolm traveled to Jeddah, Saudi Arabia, for the eventual pilgrimage to Mecca. When Malcolm arrived in Jeddah, the Saudi authorities examined his documents, including his American passport, and they refused to allow him to continue onto Mecca. The introductory letter and other credentials did not help Malcolm for various reasons, including the fact that the immigration authorities on hand at the airport did not speak or read anything in the English language. The authorities informed Malcolm that he would have to appear before what was known as the Hajj court, which would decide whether or not he was qualified to make the pilgrimage to Mecca. In the interim, he was moved to a facility, where others in a similar situation awaited a determination of their fate. Eventually, Malcolm found someone who spoke English and asked him to contact Dr. Omar Azzam, a Saudi engineer whose number Malcolm had obtained from the Islamic Association before his departure from the United States. Dr. Azzam was the son of Abdel Rahman Azzam, a highly respected Egyptian scholar and politician. When Dr. Azzam learned that Malcolm had not been allowed to continue onto Mecca, he fetched Malcolm from the airport and hosted him until his appointment with the Hajj court. While there, Malcolm was treated royally by Islamic brothers and sisters with white skin. After the Hajj court determined that he was fit to enter the Islamic holy land, he was given use of a car, which took him to Mecca, where he began his pilgrimage.[15]

Malcolm's pilgrimage to Mecca was, for him, similar to a second rebirth of sorts, as it was his initial introduction to orthodox Islam. The first instance of a similar importance or situation for him took place while Malcolm was still in jail, where he became acquainted with Islamic teachings through his two older brothers, and he eventually converted to Islam. As he learned, the pilgrimage involved several acts of obedience that were to be engaged in by all true Muslims. First, he had to take off his sandals and perform ablutions before he entered the great mosque or Kaa'ba that contains a cube-like stone edifice that orthodox Muslims recognize as the House of God. Second, Malcolm completed seven prescribed circumambulations of the Kaa'ba, along with thousands of other Muslims who were on a similar journey. Third, Malcolm drank from the 140-foot deep Well of Zamam, which served as a source of refuge for Hagar, as she looked for water for herself and Abraham's son Ishmael. Fourth, Malcolm followed the original path that Hagar took as she looked for water, seven times as a way of commemorating her frantic search.[16]

From there, Malcolm enthusiastically traveled to the Mount of Mercy, an elevated area where the Islamic prophet Muhammad had preached his farewell sermon. There, Malcolm joined thousands of Islamic pilgrims, who were encamped in tents, and they prayed from noon to sunset. This lengthy prayer time is recognized as the zenith of the pilgrimage for Islamic believers. The final rite that Malcolm participated in was the hurling of seven stones at the pillars that are said to mark the place where the devil unsuccessfully tempted Abraham. The pillars represent the devil and the hurling of the stones was an act that symbolized Allah's victory over the devil. For Malcolm, the pilgrimage seemed to represent more than the acts of obedience. It also represented a true understanding of orthodox Islam, which he believed empowered him with the knowledge and credentials to reignite his leadership status in the United States among black Muslims. After Malcolm completed the pilgrimage, he met with Prince Faisal of Saudi Arabia and was given the privileges of a guest of state, which included the best lodging, chauffeur-driven cars, and an audience with the prince.[17]

Before leaving Saudi Arabia, Malcolm sent correspondence—made up of postcards and airmail letters—to many people back in the United States. In such correspondence, he informed his family members, friends, and supporters about his pilgrimage as well as the religious and racial conversion that had taken him from the NOI leader Muhammad's version of Islam to what he felt was a true understanding of orthodox Islam since his arrival in the Middle East. Also, he was amazed by several events in the 11 days when he was taking part in events of the Muslim world. For example, Malcolm was fascinated by the fact that, as a Muslim, he had eaten from the same plates, drunk from the same glasses, and shared the same beds (or the same praying rugs) with other Islamic nationalities while praying to the same God (or Allah) with fellow Muslims from different parts of the world. He also saw how the Muslims he met on the pilgrimage were not necessarily blacks but very different human beings, including those with different hair texture and skin color. It was at the time that he felt, as Dr. King often used to say in his sermons, that all persons are children of God, who is called Allah by Muslims.[18]

Malcolm claimed that these interactions with Muslims of different nationalities and ethnicities, including white men and women, forced him to revise his thinking about nonblacks, including whites. The experience had allowed him to share a spirit of brotherhood with white men and women that he thought was previously unthinkable. His stay in Saudi Arabia ended, and he departed for a brief stay in Beirut, followed by a three-week tour of Africa, including revisiting Nigeria, Liberia, Senegal, Algeria, and Ghana. During his time visiting those places, he continued to educate himself about orthodox Islam as well as gave lectures on college and university campuses and met with the leaders in those countries.[19] Malcolm considered his visits to Nigeria and Ghana as highlights of his trip to the motherland, as he often liked to call the continent. In both countries, he was able to meet important political and Islamic leaders, including Kwame Nkrumah of Ghana, whom he considered to be a true pan-Africanist.[20]

On May 21, 1964, Malcolm X returned to the United States via Kennedy International Airport in New York, where he was met by a large crowd of supporters as well as news reporters, who had apparently learned about his new religious conversion as a Sunni Muslim and his change in racial doctrine. There, on that day at the airport, the largest news conference in which Malcolm X had ever been involved took place. It gave him the opportunity to inform his fellow Americans and also the world of his renaissance (or rebirth) as a Sunni Muslim, who now believed in orthodox Islam, coupled with his new understanding that not all white people were devils. His trip to Africa had also given him a new perspective on the nationalist struggles of various countries on the continent, which had attained their independence from colonial rule. In those former colonial nations, Malcolm saw how proud the citizens and their leaders were, and he dwelt on that at his press conference, describing it as having experienced true black pride. The press conference and Malcolm's careful answers to questions also served as a vehicle in his efforts to remake himself from being seen as only the former protégé or the follower of the Honorable Elijah Muhammad of the NOI, what some writers, including Columbia University professor Manning Marable, have referred to as a life of reinvention.[21]

As Malcolm X expected, his post-Mecca persona was the beginning of a new public image, whereby he was seen as a religious leader in his own right. He used the opportunity to reiterate his break from the NOI and, this time, also to announce the formation of the Organization of African-American Unity (OAAU). He planned to use this organization as a vehicle through which he would promote black pride, unity, and several aspects of his political ambitions. He was also glad to announce that while he was in Africa, his young organization the MMI had been admitted as a member of the Islamic Federation of the United States and Canada.[22]

Malcolm X's views, at this point, were radically changed. For example, he ceased to castigate whites because, in Saudi Arabia, he realized that not only blacks were Muslims, but that members of the Islamic faith came from all racial shades and colors. Such a new thinking on the part of Malcolm X would not be tolerated by his former brothers and sisters in the NOI, including his former mentor, Muhammad. Although Muhammad and the leadership of their black Islamic group did not openly show hostility to Malcolm X for altering his view of whites, it was still obvious that he had placed himself in an awkward and dangerous position. What became clear, at the time, was that several actions of the federation, to which Malcolm's MMI had become a member, had a direct effect on the NOI and its daily operations. Those actions of the federation made it difficult for the NOI to develop any new initiatives, and the NOI was unable to continue dealings with the orthodox Islamic world. Malcolm was, therefore, seen as a major threat to Muhammad's organization. Therefore, it was not surprising that on September 1, 1964, Judge Maurice Wahl of New York circuit court issued a pro-NOI court ruling that ordered Malcolm X and his entire family to leave their home in the Queens area of New York to return the property to its rightful owner, the NOI. According to the order, Malcolm had time until January 31, 1965, to leave the house.[23]

It was also at the time that the Federal Bureau of Investigation (FBI) and the Central Intelligence Agency (CIA) were looking into several reports about Malcolm's utterances and actions in the Middle East and Africa during his 1964 overseas trip, during which he performed the *hajj* and visited several African countries. They were trying to ascertain as to whether or not Malcolm X, while abroad, signed any protocols with foreign entities that would violate the Logan Act, a law that made it illegal for American citizens to enter into unauthorized agreements with foreign nations. These measures were to make room for the FBI and the American legal authorities to find a way to arrest and prosecute Malcolm upon his return to the United States from his overseas trip, but nothing adverse came out of these investigations. Malcolm was left alone to deal with his problems with Muhammad and his cronies, who were trying to get him out of his residence.[24]

Also, during this period, Malcolm X took time to draw a comparison between what the NOI was still doing publicly and the activities of his new MMI as well as its political wing, the OAAU. That was imperative because in Malcolm's opinion, it was a fact that, in its practice of black separatism, the NOI—from which Malcolm had disassociated himself—did preach black pride, just as he had started to preach it within his two new organizations. Yet, in Malcolm's view, what the NOI tried to preach to its members about black pride was seen mostly in rhetorical terms. Instead, upon his return from Africa, Malcolm took his interpretation of black pride further by working to put the slogan into action.

While in Africa, Malcolm happily had the opportunity to attend several meetings, including the 1964 annual meeting of the then OAU in Egypt, attended only by black leaders. In fact, it was during that meeting that he had initially met several pan-Africanist leaders, including Ghana's president Kwame Nkrumah, Tanzania's president Julius K. Nyerere, Zambia's Kenneth Kaunda, and Egypt's president Gamal Abdel Nasser, who played host to the 1964 OAU meeting. In fact, it was from one of the largest gatherings of African leaders, at the time, that Malcolm X formed the idea of returning to the United States to form the OAAU. This organization would have aspirations that were similar to those of the OAU, which was headquartered at the time in the Ethiopian capital of Addis Ababa. Historically, the OAU had been formed in Addis Ababa in 1963, amid glowing speeches by various African leaders, in which they called for the unification of the continent. This unification would serve as a vehicle to make sure that the independence that African leaders were striving for in their countries, which were former colonial entities, was real and purposeful. For example, Ghana's president Kwame Nkrumah had vowed in his inaugural speech on March 6, 1957, when Ghana attained its independence from the United Kingdom, to change its name from the Gold Coast. Nkrumah contended that the independence of Ghana was meaningless unless it was linked to the total liberation of the entire African continent. Therefore, for Malcolm X, the meeting with Nkrumah at

the OAU annual conclave of African leaders in Egypt, before he traveled to Nigeria, Ghana, and other African countries, was certainly a
historic moment for him. It was, therefore, not surprising that upon his
return to the United States, Malcolm X announced the formation of
the OAAU at his major press conference at the Kennedy International
Airport. He could use it to promote the unity and progressive development of the diaspora-based blacks, but this time, with the headquarters
of the OAAU—formed in May 1964—based in the United States.[25]

Furthermore, Malcolm X planned to use the OAAU to build link-
ages with African nationalists, especially those leaders who were still
fighting to free their countries on the African continent from colonial
domination as well as leaders of independent African countries such as
those that he met at the 1964 annual meeting of the OAU in Cairo.
At the time, Malcolm had read enough of African history to know
that such countries as Angola, Mozambique, and South Africa were
still under either outright colonial domination or were white-ruled.
About South Africa, for example, Malcolm had learned that since the
mid-1940s, the whites from the Netherlands—who called themselves
Afrikaans—had entrenched themselves in leadership positions and,
consequently, instituted what became known as an apartheid nation.
In South Africa, native blacks were relegated to the bottom of citizenship in their own country. Malcolm was appalled that such black
leaders as Nelson Mandela (the future post-apartheid South African
president), Walter Sisulu, and Steve Biko had either been imprisoned,
exiled, or assassinated. What was very interesting for Malcolm was that
most of the happenings of the colonized nations of Africa boiled down
to what Dr. W. E. B. Du Bois had discussed in his book, *The Souls of
Black Folk*, with his prediction that the problem of the 20th century
would be that of the color line.[26]

Malcolm's two new organizations began to promote black pride
through pan-Africanism, just as he and other black leaders of his generation had become very much aware of the fact that Jamaica-born
Marcus Garvey had established his own brand of black organization
known as the Universal Negro Improvement Association (UNIA),
whose sole aim was to bring about the liberation of the black race and
also for blacks to start thinking about Africa as their ancestral home.
Malcolm, whose late father was a Garvey supporter, was happy to learn

that Garvey had later on founded an African Communities League within his UNIA to create the Universal Negro Improvement Association and African Communities League (UNIA-ACL). Subsequently, to back up his "Back to Africa" slogan, Garvey established the Black Star Line, a shipping agency that would operate as a shipping line to take freed slaves back to Africa. Malcolm would not go as far as to try to convince his supporters to move to Africa, as Garvey did. Yet, he preached to his audiences about the importance of pan-Africanism, which had been embraced by the Ghanaian president Kwame Nkrumah, Egyptian president Gamal Abdel Nasser, Guinean president Sekou Toure, and other black leaders from the continent.[27]

At this time, Malcolm X's public speeches and lectures on college and university campuses were seen as being well researched to include very serious or rich pieces of information. That was because during his African trip, he had come across very useful pieces of information that he had kept to be included in such speeches. For example, he had become very much aware that such 20th-century radical leaders as Prince Hall (leader of Prince Hall Masons), Martin Delany, Edward Wilmot Blyden, and Henry Highland Garnet had been operating in collaboration with Du Bois and various pan-African leaders that Malcolm met in Egypt in 1964. Such African leaders, in speaking with Malcolm X, had advocated for the involvement of the African diaspora in African affairs back on the continent. Therefore, when Malcolm formed his OAAU, he did so to resurrect the legacy of Garvey's movement, which uniquely sought to advance a pan-African philosophy that would inspire a global mass movement for economic empowerment that focused on Africa but with Garveyism as its cornerstone. Although Garvey was no longer in the United States, Malcolm still became aware that Garveyism, like the Nkrumaism of Ghana's president Kwame Nkrumah, inspired such movements as the NOI, pan-Africanism, and the Rastafarian movement of the Caribbean nations that also saw Garvey and Ethiopian emperor Haile Selassie as being among their heroes, or religiously, prophets. Malcolm was fascinated by the fact that Ethiopian emperor Haile Selassie, one of the OAU leaders on the African continent that he had met in Cairo in 1964, was considered the titular head and mentor of the Rastafarian movement of the Caribbean. These Caribbean-based members of the Rastafarian movement traveled each

year on their annual pilgrimage to Ethiopia, while Muslims went to
Mecca and other holy cities in the Middle East.[28]

During this time of the Cold War era, many of the post-independent
African leaders, Caribbean radical leaders like Garvey, and other U.S.-
based black leaders, including Dr. Du Bois, were known to ascribe to
socialism. This also included what they described as African socialism. Yet, Malcolm X was never known to share those beliefs. Instead,
Malcolm had fraternal friendships with several political leaders of Africa and the Caribbean as well as the black diaspora, but he was never
interested in the socialist slogans that some of the other black leaders
shouted politically. Therefore, many Americans were not surprised that
upon his return from Africa to America, Malcolm X held a press conference at the airport to announce the establishment of the OAAU,
which had aspirations that were similar to what the OAU had, but
he never showed any interest in any ideologies that African leaders
preached. Malcolm had the staunch support of several black intellectuals, including John Henrik Clarke, the historian, and the OAAU name
was given to Malcolm's second new organization.[29]

In his writings, Malcolm X did laud the genuine freedom and happi-
ness that he saw among independent African nations and their black
leaders, compared to the caution exercised by such black leaders as
the Rev. Dr. Martin Luther King, Jr. and other civil rights leaders of
America. In fact, in comparison to what he saw in African liberation
struggles, Malcolm went to the extent of ridiculing the American
civil rights movement and its leaders. He asked them to travel to the
African continent or the motherland to learn about how black leaders, including the leaders of nationalist liberation movements on the
continent, were willing to shed blood to make sure that they received
their freedom. In fact, he bemoaned the fact that it was only in the
civil rights movement of America, in its struggle for freedom, that men
and women would link up arms, sing Negro Spirituals, and also call for
nonviolence, as Dr. King and his followers were adhering to Mohandas
Gandhi's philosophy of nonviolence.[30]

In his earlier public lectures, Malcolm had shown admiration for how
Gandhi and other Indian nationalists worked very hard to drive away
the British colonial leaders from India, but not necessarily for what
Dr. King described as the Gandhian philosophy of nonviolence.

Malcolm X deep in thought during a press conference in 1964. (Library of Congress)

Malcolm had shown in his teachings to new Islamic converts that it was a historical fact that in India's search for freedom or independence from the British colonial authorities, Gandhi urged his fellow countrymen and women that since British military might was much stronger than their own, the best avenue to reach their goal for freedom was through nonviolence. That, in Malcolm's view, did not mean that the American civil rights movement and its leaders of the 1960s should also adhere to similar tactics, especially at the time when such racist white leaders as Alabama governor George Wallace and others were using police dogs and violent tactics to stop peaceful civil rights marches led by Dr. King and others. Before Malcolm left the NOI, he was ready to meet white force with black force in his search for civil and human rights in America, just as Nkrumah of Ghana, Kenyatta of Kenya, Nyerere of Tanzania, and other African leaders did in their efforts to drive away colonial leaders.[31]

As things stood among the main black organizations in America—popularly and collectively known as the civil rights movement—Malcolm X saw that several black leaders and even young blacks had been maimed or killed without justification. He particularly had in mind Medgar Evers, the field organizer of the National Association for the Advancement of Colored People (NAACP), who was shot and killed in cold blood, but his accused killer was initially freed by an all-white jury. Therefore, he could not adhere to a nonviolence philosophy, which expected black men and women to stand with their hands behind their backs when their children were being bombed to death in churches in the 1960s, as was done in Alabama at a Baptist Church, or when police dogs were sent to maul and disrupt peaceful demonstrators, with water hoses turned on them at the instigation of such public officials as Governor George Wallace of Alabama in the face of governmental inaction on the part of the administration of President John F. Kennedy.[32] It was the same period, in the 1960s, that several black leaders were murdered in America, including Medgar Evers, who was reportedly shot dead in 1964 by Byron de Beckwith in Mississippi but, as black leaders of the time claimed, "was never convicted."[33]

Malcolm X did not also believe in the notion that black leaders should remain peaceful and nonviolent when their children were being mistreated on elementary school and college campuses simply because they wanted to attend the decent schools that white children attended. Malcolm was aware of the fact that there was, at the time, separate but unequal schools for blacks and whites—an unconstitutional arrangement that was supposed to have been ended by *Brown v. Board of Education of Topeka (Kansas)*. In this 1954 Supreme Court case, the Justices ruled that the separate and unequal notion of providing education to black and white children was unconstitutional.

A major issue was that Malcolm and other black leaders knew that black children were intimidated and ridiculed if they sought to attend educational institutions earmarked only for whites. It was a fact at the time that Alabama governor George Wallace took it upon himself to go and stand in the doorway of a school in Alabama to affirm that segregation would continue in his southern state at the time, tomorrow, and in future. Also, blacks and their leaders saw partial victory when the U.S. Supreme Court ended separate and unequal educational institutions in *Brown v. Board of Education of Topeka* and public transportation use for blacks after the 1955 Montgomery bus boycott. What continued to exist was that leaders who fought for these rights that ushered into existence such civil rights, including the young Martin Luther King, Jr., and Malcolm X, did not live to enjoy them. Instead, both leaders were murdered at the age of 39.[34]

During this time of hectic organizational activities for his two new organizations, Malcolm X was very much irritated by what was going on in the United States with regard to race relations. That was why he underscored unequivocally and surprisingly that, politically, there was no difference between Alabama's segregationist Governor Wallace and Mr. Lyndon B. Johnson, who had succeeded assassinated president John F. Kennedy in November 1963 as the president of the United States.[35] Most importantly, Malcolm X was delighted that apart from the MMI, which was to be used for his religious interests, his new political organization, the OAAU, would provide him with the non-partisan political platform to enter the fray to provide an alternative vision for black liberation in America, similar to how leaders of Africa's OAU had succeeded in getting political independence for their countries. It was, therefore, not surprising that Malcolm X and his supporters in the OAAU felt that the charter of the African organization "might serve as a blueprint for the OAAU."[36]

Chapter 4

INTERNATIONAL CONNECTIONS, 1964–1965

During the initial years of his leadership in the Nation of Islam, (NOI), Malcolm X was known primarily within the contexts of American racial and religious politics. However, Malcolm X's international outlook as well as interests would take a positive and an active shape starting in the fall of 1960. During that time, he had his initial opportunity to be invited to meet and hold discussions with several African, Caribbean, and Latin American leaders, who were coming to New York to attend the annual General Assembly of the United Nations (UN). As the head of NOI's Temple No. 7 in Harlem, Malcolm was readily available to meet with several international dignitaries. At a moment's notice, he was able to accept invitations to attend diplomatic and other social receptions at the UN. Malcolm's roles in UN events would become considerably more pronounced after he launched the Organization of Afro-American Unity (OAAU) upon his break with the NOI in 1964.

As one of the very active and conspicuous black leaders in the New York area at the time, Malcolm X was selected to be part of the fall 1960s welcoming black delegation to meet foreign dignitaries during international meetings in the New York area. For example, at one of the local Harlem hotels, Malcolm and other members of the delegation formally received Cuba's then revolutionary leader, President Fidel Castro, who had used an armed insurrection to seize political power from Cuba's long-term dictator, Fulgencio Batista. At the time, the young Cuban leader was paying his first visit to New York to attend the 1960 UN General Assembly, during which he had chosen to stay at Harlem's Hotel Theresa, where he would meet with Malcolm and the other local black leaders. Malcolm was so proud of the honor of meeting with Castro that when, in later years, he visited Africa, he made sure to remind the Cuban diplomats at local Cuban Embassies in Ghana, Nigeria, and other countries that when their leader visited Harlem in the fall of 1960, he had an audience with him.

The period between 1960 and 1965 was also an opportunity for Malcolm to meet several African leaders, including the then leaders of Ghana (President Kwame Nkrumah), Egypt (President Gamal Abdel Nasser), Zambia (President Kenneth Kaunda), Guinea (President Sekou Toure), and several others. Malcolm X's interest in these leaders was two-fold: first, they were leaders from continental Africa with much

Malcolm X addressing a crowd gathered at a rally in New York City, ca. 1960. (AP Photo)

experience from their anticolonial backgrounds; and second, they were champions of the anticolonialist as well as antiapartheid struggles that were taking place on the African continent.[1]

The fall 1960 meeting in Harlem of Malcolm and other black leaders with Cuba's Castro was part of ongoing interactions of black leaders with the Cuban leader. Since Batista's overthrown regime was very close to the U.S. government of President Eisenhower, the administration promptly made it known publicly that the new Cuban regime of Castro would not be recognized. Therefore, the Eisenhower government adopted several measures to undermine and, if possible, to destabilize Castro's leadership of Cuba.

Several black intellectuals from the United States did not side with the Eisenhower regime, which had Richard Nixon, a former conservative Republican senator from California, as its vice president. Malcolm was aware that Castro enjoyed the support of such black writers as John Henrik Clarke, Harold Cruse, LeRoi Jones (who changed his name in the 1960s to Amiri Baraka), Julian Mayfield, Robert Williams, and James Baldwin. Together with other nonblack leading intellectuals like C. Wright Mills, I. F. Stone, and Allen Ginsberg, the black writers formed the pro-Castro group known as the Fair Play for Cuba Committee. In June 1960, the committee sponsored a trip to Cuba for Williams, who was asked to encourage Castro to plan a visit to the United States, and the best opportunity was during the UN General Assembly, which brought Castro to Harlem in the fall of 1960. Malcolm, who was not part of the committee for religious reasons, still remained positive about Cuba, as he and several others felt cordial toward its leader, Castro.[2]

Malcolm X and other radical black leaders—including several of the writers named earlier—had succeeded in making very meaningful contacts with several leaders of the developing world at the UN, including President Castro of Cuba. Therefore, Malcolm and some of the black leaders of the United States had planned to request an appearance before the UN Decolonization Committee to bring their complaints about lack of civil and human rights for the United States–based blacks before the world body. Malcolm, who knew very well the UN's Undersecretary-General and Nobel Peace Prize laureate Ralph Bunche, had plans to enlist the assistance of Dr. Bunche in that endeavor. The strategy did not sit well with the Eisenhower administration because, at the time, the American government was privately courting several of the emergent new African leaders in whose countries American companies were getting lucrative business and other developmental contracts. For example, during a 1960 visit to Washington, D.C., Ghanaian president Nkrumah had the chance to meet with President Eisenhower to appeal for assistance in building for Ghana the country's first major hydroelectric dam for electrification purposes. The project, when completed, was to benefit Ghana and its neighboring West African nations that sorely needed electricity. The 1960 visit by Nkrumah was as a result of his meeting in Accra with then U.S. vice president Richard Nixon at the March 6, 1957, independence day celebration of Ghana, during which Mr. Nixon also first met with the Reverend Dr. Martin Luther King, Jr., the civil rights activist. It was at that time, too, that a formal invitation was extended for the new Ghanaian leader to visit the United States. Consequently, the American Valco Aluminum Company got the contract to build Ghana's Volta River Project, which included the hydroelectric dam at Akosombo as well as the largest man-made lake created for recreational sports and other purposes out of the Volta River, from which large-scale fishing takes place even today—projects that Malcolm X visited when he went to Ghana.[3]

In the context of pan-Africanism, whereby African leaders and black leaders of the diaspora sought to forge black unity on an international scale, many of these leaders considered it to be very important to their relationship with Malcolm X as a black leader in the United States. That was why they interacted with him cordially at very high levels, a situation which had helped Malcolm to know some of them personally. Therefore, by 1964, it became very easy for Malcolm X to embark on foreign travels that took him to African nations after paying religious visits to the Middle East. In reciprocity, Malcolm X attached so much importance to his relations with black leaders in Africa as well as his travels on the continent that he did not allow anything, including his lack of financial resources, to thwart his ambitions. To be able to obtain a ticket to travel, he accepted a personal loan from his half-sister Ella to make possible his 1964 trips to the Middle East and, later, to several African nations. Observers like University of Michigan professor Kevin Gaines and others felt that the pilgrimage did enrich Malcolm's understanding of Islam as a universalizing world religion.[4]

Apart from the spiritual aspects of Malcolm's overseas trips at the time, he also had a political agenda, whereby he planned to make known to various African and Middle Eastern leaders the plight of his fellow blacks back in the United States. However, he faced an uphill task in his earlier quest to use the trips to humiliate American leaders through his international contacts, especially as he sought to advertise widely the plight of his fellow blacks wherever he visited. He made it seem that only American whites were to be blamed for the subordinate or underclass status of blacks. When Malcolm did not receive instant support that he had hoped for his anti-American views and claims of racism against his fellow blacks from African leaders, he started to equate racism in America to the apartheid conditions that prevailed in South Africa. In documents that he circulated among African leaders when he was visiting the African continent and also among African diplomats at the UN headquarters in New York, Malcolm wrote emphatically that "the racism that blacks faced in America was the same that it is in South Africa."[5] Malcolm X was surprised that African leaders who treated him like one of their own and referred to him as a brother, especially during his trips to their countries, were during this time around very lukewarm in embracing his quest for their support against the United States. Malcolm X was publicly honored during his sojourns in Africa, and he was affectionately received in many places. For example, he was invited to speak on major academic campuses, including the premier Nigerian academic institution known as the University of Ibadan, which had prestigious affiliations with the University of London and Cambridge University in the United Kingdom. Although foreigners were not very much welcome in several African countries soon after postcolonial rule, Malcolm was always well received. For example, he was also made an honorary member of the Nigerian Muslim Students' Association. At the reception honoring him, the indigenous Nigerian leaders present bestowed upon him the indigenous Yoruba name of "*Omowale*," which meant that he was like the lost son, who had come back home (in the Yoruba language of Western Nigeria). That was why Malcolm X wrote in his autobiography that he had never received a more treasured honor anywhere in his life.[6]

During this time in 1964, Malcolm X started to show bitterness toward African leaders because they were not supporting his cause against the United States. In fact, Malcolm infuriated several of the African leaders when he gave the impression that the only way African leaders could demonstrate true pan-Africanism was for them to condemn the United States for what Malcolm considered to be the United States' violations of black human rights back home. He added that it was his fervent hope that the African leaders—whom he called his brothers—had not escaped the domination of Europe, only to fall victim to what he described as "American dollarism."[7] Malcolm had also failed, at the 1964 OAU meeting in Cairo, to get African leaders to condemn the United States.

Malcolm X thought that he might have more political success with East African leaders than he did with West African and northern African leaders. Therefore, on October 5, 1964, he flew to the Kenyan capital of Nairobi, where he started with a relaxing visit to a national safari park, after which he contacted the office of Vice President Oginga Odinga. Malcolm's strategy had always been to ingratiate himself with the customs and traditions of Africa whenever he arrived in an African country. He also tried to understand indigenous or tribal/ethnic matters. Therefore, he was happy to learn that Vice President Odinga belonged to Kenya's second dominant ethnic (or tribal) group known as the Luo, which was second in size to the ruling Kikuyu ethnic group, to which Kenyan president Jomo Kenyatta belonged. Malcolm was glad that, in Kenya, he had the opportunity to meet President Kenyatta and several of his top cabinet members. When he was in Kenya, Malcolm was able to visit and hold discussions with Odinga as well as Kenyan leaders like Tom Mboya, who was later assassinated in cold blood in a Kenyan street. When he paid a quick visit to the neighboring Republic of Tanzania, Malcolm X met a fellow Muslim by the name of Muhammad Babu, who was an important political leader from the island of Zanzibar. Babu made sure that Malcolm paid a courtesy visit to the office of President Julius K. Nyerere of Tanzania, during which he held fraternal discussions with him. From Tanzania, he flew to the Republic of Uganda, where he held meetings with President Milton Apollo Obote and other political leaders in that country. Obote's government would later be overthrown by the military dictator, Gen. Idi Amin Dada, an event that forced Dr. Obote to escape from Uganda to live in exile in Tanzania, as the guest of President Nyrerere.[8]

Malcolm X, then recent founder of the Organization of Afro-American Unity (OAAU) and the Muslim Mosque Inc. (MMI), meeting with Abdulrahman M. Babu, former Minister of State in the United Republic of Tanganyika and Zanzibar (now part of Tanzania), in Dar-es-Salaam in October 1964. (AP Photo)

Although Malcolm X was far away from New York, he still felt very concerned about his two organizations: the MMI and the OAAU. While he was doing what he loved best to do, which included traveling extensively and drawing international attention, he still missed the kinship and sense of purpose that he found in working with these organizations. He was still aware of the fact that for the several weeks he had been traveling outside of the United States in 1964, it was his inexperienced followers who took over leadership of the organizations and made efforts to fashion Malcolm's message as well as his mission. On November 23, 1964, Malcolm was on his way back to the United States from Africa when he stopped in Paris to give a lecture and to visit places of interest, including university campuses. A week later, on November 30, 1964, Malcolm flew to the United Kingdom, where he participated in a British Broadcasting Corporation (BBC)–televised debate at the famous Oxford Union that took place on December 3, 1964. The topic of the debate was "Extremism in the Defense of Liberty Is No Vice, and Moderation in the Pursuit of Justice Is No Virtue."[9]

Malcolm's international invitations grew steadily, as he was invited on February 8, 1965, to speak in London before the first meeting of the Council of African Organizations (CAO). However, when he tried to enter France on February 9, 1965, to give a speech in Paris, he was shocked that the French immigration authorities at an airport near Paris refused him entry, which had not happened before. He, therefore, flew back to London, and on February 12, he visited the Birmingham area of the United Kingdom. This area had become very volatile racially after the 1964 British general elections, in which the Conservative Party won the area's parliamentary seat. Since Malcolm's overseas sojourns, several writers and researchers of the U.S. civil rights struggle have used his travels as a yardstick to measure Malcolm X's effectiveness as a black leader as well as his impressive international credentials. The credentials included all of the aforementioned junkets, lectures, and extensive travels inside Africa that took place between 1964 and 1965.[10]

To some scholars back in the United States, Malcolm's internationalization of the local struggles of various black organizations did represent a pan-African variant that he seemed to appreciate, understand and, indeed, promote. Malcolm embarked on that route on the basis of his previous vow to use "any means necessary" that would further the struggle of blacks for civil rights, equality, and equity, irrespective of the cost. Given his prevailing international outlook as well as his earlier revolutionary outlook, Malcolm was seen by radical black leaders as being more purposeful than other civil rights leaders, who preached peaceful ways of doing things as opposed to the violent or motive force that Malcolm and others preached. Yet, it was clear to observers of Malcolm and Dr. King that, indeed, both black leaders wanted to win freedom for their black constituencies, even if by differing methods.[11]

In Malcolm X's opinion, international or regional organizations like the UN and the Africa-based Organization for African Unity (OAU)—which is now called the Africa Union (AU)—should have the moral duty to assist the black leaders of the United States in their quest for civil and human rights. Malcolm X felt that it was only unfortunate that Dr. Ralph Bunche, as an international civil servant and an Undersecretary-General of the UN, was not ready to be counted on or used to further the cause of his fellow blacks in the United States. When Malcolm and others were very busy in the 1950s on the national front to publicize the cause of U.S. blacks at conferences organized by African leaders and UN, Dr. Bunche had been assigned to work on Israeli–Palestinian peace efforts in the Middle East. These efforts would win for Bunche the Nobel Peace Prize, the international honor that would much later also be awarded to Dr. King in 1964 for his own pioneering leadership in the U.S. civil rights movement. Many black leaders as well as several international leaders at the time felt that Dr. Bunche, who had been serving in the second leadership position of the UN since August 9, 1954, deserved the Oslo-based Peace Prize.[12]

Several black and nonblack leaders like Dr. King, Rev. Ralph Abernathy, A. Philip Randolph, and Jewish leaders, who were observing Malcolm X's utterances and writings between 1964 and 1965, felt that he was being unduly influenced by foreign forces due to his overseas travels. There were those who saw him as drifting toward socialism and even Marxism. In fact, conspiracy theorists in the United States saw Malcolm as representing a direct threat to the country's security interests. It was during this time that Malcolm offered his public support to U.S. Socialist Workers Party presidential candidate Clifton DeBerry, while Malcolm at the same time agreed to accept invitations from the Militant Labor Forum (MLF) to give some of his radical speeches. All of such moves made some leaders of the American security forces, including Federal Bureau of Investigation (FBI) director J. Edgar Hoover, consider Malcolm as moving toward socialism and that he was a threat to the United States' national security.[13]

When members of the large audiences that Malcolm addressed tried to find out, through questioning, his ideological or political leanings, Malcolm was not very helpful at all, as he proved to be vague. For example, in his response to one such question, Malcolm tried to answer in parables. He answered that he did not actually have a direct answer about his ideological leanings, as he claimed that he did not know. Yet, he added that he was flexible about such ideological and political leanings. Malcolm went on to point out that most of the colonized countries, which were fighting to throw off their colonial shackles or what he considered to be oppression, were embracing socialism, adding: "I don't think it is an accident."[14]

Malcolm X, as some authors have concluded in their writings about him, did attract the attention and even scrutiny of American political leaders as well as security agencies, including the FBI when he was in the United States and by the Central Intelligence Agency (CIA) as he traveled overseas. As one writer observed, Malcolm made strenuous efforts to turn newly independent African nations against the American government of the day, regardless of which political party (i.e., Republican Party or Democratic Party) was in power. Some independent observers believe that if Malcolm had succeeded in his efforts to make African countries and their leaders antagonistic toward the United States and its leaders in the midst of the Cold War, that "could have serious repercussions."[15]

As explained by several writers, there were varied reasons why such foregoing anti-American activities on the part of Malcolm in Africa would have been problematic for the United States' diplomatic goals and even image. For example, it was known that all major countries of the world in the ideological West and East at the time—including the United States—endeavored to court the newly freed European colonies of Africa so that these foreign nations could continue to have access to the continent's abundant natural and human resources. Malcolm was aware of the fact that similar ambitions, some centuries ago, led to the introduction of the slave trade by European traders and, to a lesser extent, by the Arabs before its abolition in the United States through President Abraham Lincoln's Emancipation Proclamation. While Malcolm X felt that there was nothing good or moral about the way the United States–based blacks were being treated by whites with respect to racism, the United States Information Agency (USIA) Director Carl Rowan, as a black diplomat, tried his best to dilute Malcolm X's anti-American attacks by pointing to some of the accomplishments back home, including the1964 Civil Rights Act, as a truly positive step in the right direction, especially in the struggle for equality in the United States. Director Rowan, who later on wrote widely distributed syndicated columns, and others were able to explain to African leaders that Malcolm X had overblown the issues at stake and that they should never trust or believe him. Since Rowan was also black, some African leaders took his words seriously.[16]

Due to the aggressive way that Malcolm was presenting his information to postcolonial African leaders like Nkrumah (Ghana), Kenyatta

(Kenya), Toure (Guinea), Modibo Keita (Mali), Nyerere (Tanzania), Kenneth Kaunda (Zambia), and others, several of them did take him seriously and even believed what he was saying. Subsequently, the U.S. Justice Department started a rigorous investigation of Malcolm's finances to see if he was receiving any foreign assistance and, if so, then Malcolm was to be required to register under the Foreign Agents' Registration Act. If it could be proved that he was serving any foreign interests and he had failed to register under the act, he could be arrested, charged with a felony, and punished. Among his friends and business associates interviewed by the U.S. Justice Department officials was Alex Haley, who was collaborating with him on his autobiography. The interview was for the Civil Rights Division of the Justice Department to find out if Malcolm was receiving any foreign funding. One serious rumor was that Egypt's President Gamal Abdel Nasser, as suspected from their friendship, had funneled money to the OAAU, but the FBI, which conducted the investigations, showed that "nothing of this nature was discovered."[17]

The U.S. government and its officials were irritated by Malcolm's deliberate plans to embarrass or condemn the United States at international conferences that he attended or through the foreign leaders with whom he had exchanged correspondence. The major newspapers published reports about how the American authorities were seriously scrutinizing Malcolm's life from the militant Muslim years. For example, on August 13, 1964, the New York Times reported in an article that the U.S. Department of State was working hard to gain information about Malcolm's African connections, especially in his efforts to instigate those leaders against the American government and its interests and leaders. What was to be stopped or counteracted by American diplomats was Malcolm's global claims that blacks in America were being persecuted and, as a result, he wanted the whole country censured at the UN and also in other international forums. As it was reported in several quarters, the American leaders did everything possible to make sure that Malcolm X would not succeed in his external efforts to make the United States become an international pariah like apartheid South Africa.[18]

What seemed to be helpful to the United States was the fact that Malcolm X could not succeed in his efforts to get any newly independent

African nation to agree to take to the UN his claim that blacks in America were being persecuted by the American government and its officials. The failure for Malcolm to do so stemmed from the fact that, as it was very clear at the time, the African nations that he tried to persuade already had enough problems of their own. Also, they considered the United States to be too powerful to be treated that way. In contrast, such African leaders as Nkrumah, Kenyatta, Nyerere, Toure, Keita, and Kenyatta, at the time, were willing to confront South Africa as they saw the apartheid nation as a mere regional power that could be tackled or handled that way, including confronting it at the UN and other world forums to make sure that it was kicked out of events, including international sporting events. At the time, Malcolm even threatened to bring the United States to the International Court of Justice on charges of racism against blacks but such plans on his part against the U.S. government "never got off the ground."[19]

The American officials knew very well all the strenuous efforts of Malcolm to utilize his connections in Africa to embarrass the government, especially during African continental conferences. Such anti-American activities on the part of Malcolm made him to be seen as Washington's black Public Enemy Number One, especially as he endeavored to let African leaders feel that the Negro problem in the United States, including racism, should be deemed as the problem of African leaders as well. Instead, Malcolm was simply seen as making rhetorical threats, and it was felt that he could not do very much to threaten American security. As Manning Marable wrote, Malcolm in the end failed to persuade any African leader to take his cause, not for any major flaw in his argument or the fading of his passion, but rather that Malcolm's "rhetoric simply could not overcome the cold logic of international politics."[20]

Manning wrote the following text about Malcolm X's second visit to Nigeria and the intrigue of the Nigeria–Biafra civil war:

From Kenya, Malcolm X traveled to the Ethiopian capital of Addis Ababa, which was the headquarters of the Organization for African Unity (OAU). Since he had been in that country before, Malcolm simply paid visits to the leaders of the OAU, but he did not plan to stay there very long. Instead, he made travel plans to pay a second visit to Nigeria, where he had plans, this time, to meet several of the political leaders, including President Nnamdi Azikiwe. The president had studied in the United States, first at Howard University, and later at Lincoln University in Pennsylvania, from where he earned his first degree before studying at the University of Pennsylvania. A member of the dominant Igbo ethnic group, Dr. Azikiwe was known to have influenced several West African leaders, including Ghanaian President Kwame Nkrumah, to travel to the United States to study at Historically Black Colleges and Universities (HBCUs), including his own *alma mater* in Pennsylvania, Lincoln University. Upon his arrival in Lagos, the then capital of Nigeria, Malcolm was preparing to have dinner when he received a phone call from the executive secretary to President Azikiwe, who was making the phone call to arrange a private meeting the next day with the Nigerian leader.[21]

When Malcolm first visited Nigeria, he met mostly with student leaders and heads of social organizations. Therefore, during this second visit to the oil-rich country, in late October 1964, Malcolm X was thrilled that he would have an opportunity to meet some of the nationalist leaders, who had led the country's anticolonialist struggle against the United Kingdom and, in 1960, succeeded in achieving independence for their country. From discussions with the Nigerian president, Malcolm X realized that Dr. Azikiwe had a good grasp of American black leadership, especially those who were key players in the civil rights movement. In further discussions with Dr. Azikiwe, Malcolm learned that Nigeria was a country with many problems of its own, including confrontations among the country's various ethnic or tribal groups. Malcolm was, therefore, apprehensive about Nigeria's future stability or peace. Later on, he spoke at length about what he saw to be serious problems of Nigeria, the oil-rich country that needed stability to succeed in the world. Malcolm's uneasiness was borne out by the fact that less than two years after this meeting with President Azikiwe, a bloody military coup d'état took place in Nigeria on January 15, 1966, in which the executive head of state (Prime Minister Alhaji Sir Tafawa Balewa) and several of the country's traditional as well as political leaders were murdered in cold blood by a section of the Nigerian armed forces. By 1969, Nigeria faced a secession by the then eastern region, an enclave of Igbos and their leaders. The upheavals led to a counter-coup, in which several Igbo military and political leaders were killed by military leaders from Nigeria's predominantly Hausa-Fulani ethnic groups—events which would prompt the Igbo leaders, led by then Col. O. Ojukwu, to declare a new Republic of Biafra.[22]

According to Manning, this was Malcolm X's opinion on the role of women in the OAAU:

> Malcolm X had so much admiration for Africa, which he often described as the "motherland," that he spent 24 weeks there between April and November 1964. He knew that he had the responsibility of running two organizations—the MMI and the OAAU—and to make sure that they successfully recruited new members so that they would grow. Yet, he left their running with his followers and top aides, who served as his assistants. When he returned to the United States, Malcolm realized that there were a lot of problems in the two organizations, particularly with respect to the role that women should play in them. Malcolm knew that, in the NOI, women played second fiddle to men, although the Honorable Elijah Muhammad, as the NOI leader, paid lip service that women were the mothers of civilization, and that they should be allowed to serve in prominent roles in the NOI. Yet, as several writers and observers did comment on about the status of women in Honorable Elijah Muhammad's NOI, they knew the fact was that "women played a secondary role to men."[23]

Upon Malcolm X's return to the United States in the fall of 1964 from his long trips abroad, he seemed to have had a new perspective on how women should be treated in Islamic as well as social organizations. For example, he had seen how women were actively playing important roles in newly independent African nations like Ghana, Nigeria, and Kenya. Therefore, he had plans to be firm on issues about women's roles in the MMI and OAAU, especially after he realized that in his absence from the two organizations, his subordinates did not know how to handle the issue about women's roles or place in both of them. Malcolm was amazed to realize that there was this sort of patriarchy in his two organizations. Therefore, Malcolm had plans to do away with that, as he insisted that in the OAAU, for example, "women should have equal position to men."[24]

At this time, Malcolm's senior deputy was Martin Ferguson, who played a dominant role in the OAAU. Several male members of the organization approached Ferguson to speak out about their worries, especially with respect to Malcolm's new attitude toward women in both the OAAU and MMI. Initially, Ferguson wanted to confront Malcolm about the issue, but he hesitated. Instead, he started to explain to the members with negative attitudes toward women in a way that was in line with what Malcolm wanted. For example, he unequivocally made it clear that the women Malcolm X was bent on placing in leadership positions in the OAAU and in the MMI "were responsible [and that] they were well educated."[25]

A leading official of the Muslim Mosque, Incorporated (MMI), who still had reservations about allowing women to play leading roles in the organizations formed by Malcolm was James X, who had followed Malcolm from the NOI. He and Ferguson often had verbal arguments, sometimes specifically about women being invited as speakers as part of the official roster of speakers for events of the OAAU and the MMI. After his travels in Africa, Malcolm X returned to the two organizations with a new attitude toward several topics, including good education for the young members of the organizations. Therefore, it was very much appreciated by Malcolm that James Campbell, a South Carolina black activist in the OAAU, teamed up with Ferguson to establish what they named as a Liberation School, which initially started to hold classes for a dozen OAAU and MMI members. Also, to follow Malcolm's example of establishing a Muslim newspaper for the NOI and naming it after Muhammad as the leader and mentor, an OAAU member by the name of Peter Bailey had Malcolm's permission to establish the OAAU's first newsletter, which he named *Blacklash*. Then, to make sure that there was cultural awareness among members of the two groups Malcolm had formed, Muriel Gray of New York was appointed to lead a productive cultural arts committee. Yet, the tension between the OAAU and MMI leaders was disrupting several of the organizational plans of Malcolm. Therefore, Malcolm started to be strict with the members. For instance, one morning, he was very irritated with a member of the

OAAU who was taking a nap in a comfortable chair in the Hotel The-resa headquarters. Malcolm reportedly woke him up and demanded: "Don't you have anything to do? Go out and deliver leaflets."[26]

The young man left the hotel as if he was going to carry out Mal-colm's instructions to deliver leaflets. Instead, he never came back for several weeks. Since NOI members knew that he was in Malcolm's group, they confronted him at a train station and savagely beat him up, making him end up at a local hospital with cuts and a swollen face. During this period in 1964, the New York Police Department (NYPD) was having problems with young black activists—a situation which ex-ploded into a riot when a police officer shot and wounded James Pow-ell, one of the black youth. As part of the aftermath, OAAU and MMI leaders decided to hold a public demonstration, which precipitated what became known as the Harlem riots. At the demonstration, one of Malcolm's assistants by the name of Benjamin X urged black people to arm themselves for self-protection, adding that "Negroes should be willing to spill blood for freedom."[27]

Already, officials of the NYPD were on the streets of New York and Harlem looking for troublemakers to arrest in order to undermine the black demonstrations after Powell's shooting. They targeted Benjamin X, as the FBI and the Justice Department agents were ready to arrest and have him blamed for his speech, in which he advocated that blacks should arm themselves in order to defend themselves. They saw that as instigating the crowd to riot. However, on legal advice, he was not ar-rested as it was felt that there was not sufficient evidence for his arrest. As allies with the Socialist Workers Party as well as the Militant Labor Forum, OAAU and MMI officials spoke at each other's rallies. At this time, Malcolm X had decided to divorce his political activism from the activities of the MMI—a situation that undermined the political au-thority of the MMI. To salvage the situation, Malcolm decided to make adjustments to the platforms of the OAAU and the MMI by pursuing a strategy of bringing middle-class blacks, liberal celebrities, and intel-lectuals into the OAAU. He further felt that his growing organizations needed such people of stature as Ossie Davis, the famous actor who would later preach his eulogy; his wife, Ruby Dee; Sidney Poitier, the Academy Award–winning actor, and other black professionals as well as leaders.[28]

At this particular time, Ossie Davis and others who considered themselves as friends of Malcolm X wondered about his young family during his absence for months, mostly as he traveled to Africa and other places outside the continent. They had in mind the two occasions that he visited several African countries. In his absence, Malcolm had instructed that his wife, Betty, and children be looked after by a close associate by the name of Charles X. Kenyatta, who was affiliated with the MMI as one of its leaders. Yet, Betty still felt very vulnerable as she did not feel comfortable with Kenyatta's efforts to be close to her and her children. After all, he was not related to Malcolm's family as a kin. This was the time that Betty gave birth to the family's fourth daughter, Lumbumba Shabbazz. At the time, there were four additional mouths for Betty to feed when Malcolm was paying his second visit to Africa, yet the resources to do so were limited. The family's meager income, in Malcolm's absence, was derived from the husband's book advance as well as lecture fees and donations from generous members of the OAAU and the MMI.[29]

Betty was unhappy with the rumors that NOI agents were spreading about her. Since her husband was traveling outside the United States, she relied on Kenyatta and other MMI and OAU leaders for rides to do her shopping. Instead, the NOI operatives went to the extent of spreading false information that Betty and Kenyatta were planning to get married, and that Malcolm X was not going to return to the United States. At the time, the FBI was also using its agents to spy on Malcolm X's wife as they wanted to know all of her movements in the absence of Malcolm. Although Malcolm's enemies and detractors made it seem that he had abandoned his family during his second trip to Africa, it was still a fact that he did correspond with Betty through telegrams, letters, and even phone calls. He also gave his wife the reassurance that what he was accomplishing through his African travels would eventually benefit the entire Malcolm X family. Specifically, Malcolm informed Betty in one of his letters, "But what I am doing here [in Africa] will be more helpful to the whole family in the long run."[30]

To be helpful to her absentee husband, Betty decide to get actively involved in the OAAU and MMI activities before Malcolm returned to the United States from his second trip to Africa. Toward that end, Betty decided to host some of the meetings of the organizations at her home. Apart from open meetings with Malcolm's assistants, Betty eventually started to hold secret meetings with the security head of the MMI, Reuben X Francis. She learned that in order to get the youth involved in the activities of Malcolm's two organizations in his absence from the country, Francis had decided to begin a new youth group, which was to be known as OAAU Cadets. Betty wanted to know more about the plans in order to inform Malcolm in future telephone conversations. Instead of sitting down to talk with Betty, Francis decided to telephone from home to Betty, not knowing that the FBI was monitoring phone calls coming into Malcolm's home. Francis told Betty that the young wing, the OAAUI cadets, would function separately from the main organization, adding "because I don't want the officials to know too much about it [the cadets]."[31]

The FBI, which was monitoring activities of Malcolm X's two organizations and also his home telephone, did not decide to do anything. The reason was that FBI director J. Edgar Hoover felt that the Reverend Dr. Martin Luther King, Jr. was more dangerous than Malcolm X. After all, as its records reflected, the FBI was comfortable with the fact that Malcolm X had not led mass protests through American streets to try and incite the hatred and the wrath of white communities. Also, Malcolm X had never organized and brought a quarter of a million people to Washington, D.C., to lobby for the passage of a civil rights bill into law. If anything, the FBI knew that Malcolm X had actually opposed the march on Washington that Dr. King was leading—a move that reportedly pleased the FBI. Furthermore, it was part of the thinking of the FBI leadership that in spite of Malcolm's rhetorical language, he had not fundamentally and realistically threatened to change America profoundly, and that he did nothing to make it seem that he was ready to push white people out of power and, in the end, substitute blacks in their places.[32]

American diplomats were reporting to the U.S. Department of State that Malcolm, while traveling in Africa, was giving unfavorable speeches about the United States. Yet, Hoover, at this time, considered Dr. King more dangerous than Malcolm. Therefore, as the FBI director, Hoover started to send damaging reports about him to the White House, the Justice Department, and other organizations that handled civil rights matters, mainly to try and turn all such organizations against

Dr. King and his movement, but interestingly, not against Malcolm X. Although many whites considered Malcolm X hostile, the FBI still felt that he was more peaceful than King, and that King was a reckless lawbreaker whose actions were more dangerous and destabilizing than those of Malcolm X.[33]

By late October 1964, Malcolm had been in Africa for not less than two months and was on his way back from West Africa to the United States. At the time, it dawned on him that he had not visited Liberia. This West African country was the very place that freed American slaves had settled in and thrived as the new political leaders, who called themselves Americo-Liberians. He arrived in Liberia in the first week of November 1964 from Accra, Ghana, where he visited briefly for the second time. Malcolm received an enthusiastic welcome in Monrovia, the capital named for the American president James Monroe, who had assisted black explorers from the United States in search of a new place in West Africa for several of their manumitted slaves, long before the Emancipation Proclamation signed by President Abraham Lincoln to free most of the enslaved blacks, who also chose to migrate to Liberia.[34]

Malcolm X had heard a lot about Liberia from travelers to the country and also from some of his friends who served as diplomats at the UN in New York. Therefore, upon his arrival in the capital of Liberia, he made a purposeful effort to visit the seat of government known as the Executive Mansion, which was very much similar to the U.S. White House. There, he was introduced to the Liberian cabinet, although then president William V.S. Tubman, whose ancestors migrated from the Carolinas to Liberia, was not available for Malcolm to meet. After a three-day visit to Liberia, he was ready to leave for Conakry, the capital of Guinea, where he was treated royally by the government of President SekouToure. He was so well treated—including being chauffeured around—that Malcolm felt like a visiting head of state. Also, the Guinean leader hosted a dinner for Malcolm, which was attended by several government officials and diplomats. Malcolm knew about how President Toure had defied the French government of President Charles DeGaulle and, as a result, he was happy to visit Guinea to meet the powerful leader, Toure. As he planned to leave Guinea to return to the United States, Malcolm decided to pass through Geneva, where he arrived on November 16, 1964, and he happily visited the famous Islamic Center operated by the Muslim Brotherhood Association of Switzerland to meet some of the Islamic leaders with whom he planned to correspond upon his return to the United States. It was on November 24, 1964, that Malcolm X returned to the United States, with supporters of his OAAU and MMI at the John F. Kennedy Airport carrying welcoming placards and signs that read: "Welcome Back Home, Brother Malcolm."[35]

Chapter 5

FINAL YEAR AND HIS ASSASSINATION IN 1965

By 1965, Malcolm X felt that his life was in danger. He considered himself to be a marked person, whose life was being threatened from several directions as well as by various groups. He felt that it was due to his public pronouncements, his anti-American actions overseas, and his disassociation from the Nation of Islam (NOI) that put his life in danger at that time. Malcolm and his family were very much aware of threats against his life, and they were very worried.

It became public knowledge in the last year of Malcolm X's life that he faced opposition from various quarters, part of which came from his former colleagues in the NOI, who felt unequivocally that he had betrayed the very organization that helped in nurturing and also making him an important Islamic leader. Malcolm's bitterness against his former NOI colleagues stemmed from the fact that at the time that he was traveling in Europe, his home in Queens had become a focus of acrimony between his family and the NOI. The NOI had gone to court to lay claim to the property and, as a result, seek the ejection of Malcolm's family. In Europe, the French officials did not appreciate Malcolm's radical public utterances about prevailing minority situations in France. That was why upon his arrival at Orly Airport, near Paris, for a second visit to the

French capital, the airport immigration officials did not allow him to enter France. He felt that he had a bona fide reason to enter France, as he had been invited to give a scheduled speech at an event that was being organized by the Federation of African Students in the French capital. Upon having been refused entry into France, Malcolm X returned to the United States, via the United Kingdom. That would be his last visit to Europe. On February 14, 1965, Malcolm's family home in Queens, New York, was firebombed with Molotov cocktails thrown through the windows, an incident that took place when Malcolm and his family were fast asleep. Yet, the incident did not deter Malcolm from speaking out on matters that he considered important. For example, within 24 hours of the firebombing of his home, he agreed to travel to Detroit, his former home, to give a speech at the local Ford Auditorium.[1]

Exterior view of Malcolm X's former home, with charred furniture on the front lawn, after it was firebombed on February 14, 1965. (Library of Congress)

Malcolm's family and friends were shocked by the firebombing of his home. The reason was that many of them felt that, upon his return from his two trips to the Middle East and Africa, Malcolm seemed to have started to tone down his rhetoric against his opponents, including white people of the United States as well as his former NOI colleagues. One example of the change in Malcolm was his assertion that he had learned the truth about Islam in Mecca, and that since that time, his friends would be persons from various religious and racial persuasions, including Christians, Jews, Buddhists, Hindus, agnostics, and even atheists, adding, "I have friends, who are called capitalists, socialists and Communists."[2]

Journalists and other observers of Malcolm X's daily activities after his return from his second trip to Africa indicated that they were aware of the change in him. As one of the rare occasions in his changed life, Malcolm gladly accepted an invitation to address a racially mixed audience at the Corn Hill Methodist Church in Rochester, New York, on February 16, 1965. The topic he chose to address that day was "Land of No Hope," and the calm tone he used to answer questions seemed to suggest that his experiences abroad had broadened his perspective, although he demonstrated on some occasions, when answering some irritating questions at the Corn Hill Christian event, that he was still capable of making fiery speeches. It was five days before Malcolm's assassination, and he made it clear that from what he had learned during his overseas sojourn, he was of the opinion that the international arena did not hold anything against him as a Muslim from the United States, but that outsiders saw the United States as a land of no hope, which was the thematic topic of his speech. In trying to compare himself as well as his circumstances to his opponents outside his two organizations, Malcolm still used language that his critics considered to be demeaning and condescending. For example, after the speech, Malcolm said in a response to a reporter's question in public that he did not have the desire to get bogged down in minor arguments with individuals that he described as birdbrained or small-minded people, who happened to belong to other organizations. In retrospect, observers of Malcolm's activities, including reporters, agreed that Malcolm was not the same person that they previously knew. Some journalists recalled some of the past feuds that separated Malcolm X from the leadership of the

NOI, which dated back to November of 1963 during the assassination of U.S. president John F. Kennedy. At that time, Malcolm was basically accused by Muhammad and other NOI leaders of expressing delight at the death of the President Kennedy. Therefore, in early 1965, Malcolm wisely distanced himself from the past negative comments, which had made Muhammad and other NOI leaders describe him as being insensitive.[3]

Malcolm felt bitter about the past, as he still felt that it was unjust for his opponents in the NOI to continue to see him in negative terms. What had enraged Muhammad was that when Malcolm X was still under punishment and was not expected to comment on or to participate in any public events, Malcolm took his wife, Betty, and their children to Florida to visit Cassius Clay, the heavy-weight boxing champion, who was in a training camp to get ready for his bout against Sonny Liston. Furthermore, instead of remaining silent and inactive, as Muhammad had demanded, Malcolm X later hosted a boxing victory celebration reception for Clay, who decided at the event to change his name to an Islamic name, as he became Muhammad Ali, long after he had embraced Islam.

Although Malcolm was no longer in the NOI and tried to portray himself as a changed person, information reached Muhammad and other NOI leaders that Malcolm, even in 1965, would not leave old matters alone. Instead, he allegedly continued to spread damaging information about Muhammad and the NOI, including information about Muhammad's many illegitimate children. In a short time, people who supported the NOI told Muhammad about the negative things that Malcolm was continuing to spread about him. Malcolm's obvious anger, which prompted him to resurrect old rumors about the NOI leader, included his suspicion that the early morning hours' firebombing of his home had been done by arsonists from a rival organization. Subsequently, Malcolm did not hide the fact that he very much suspected that former NOI opponents, acting on orders from Muhammad, had carried out the firebombing of the home that the NOI leaders were trying to take back from Malcolm and his family.[4]

While the foregoing events involving Malcolm and his NOI opponents were going on within Islamic circles, there was also considerable concern in certain U.S. official quarters about Malcolm X's activities, including his suspected anti-American statements. Under today's laws in America, Malcolm's anti-American activities overseas could have had him branded as an Islamic terrorist and subject to being hunted down aggressively. Instead, like Malcolm's previous actions at the United Nations (UN), American security agencies knew that Malcolm continued to cause American leaders considerable discomfort overseas with his criticisms, his correspondence, and in meetings with African leaders. In essence, Malcolm's strenuous efforts were to turn African governments and their leaders against the United States. Being black like the African leaders, Malcolm X's influence in Africa was taken seriously by American officials, who knew that he had, by January of 1965, visited not less than a dozen African countries, and that he had also had the opportunity of talking with several African heads of state at UN functions as well as addressing their national parliaments upon his arrival in their capitals. As he had in mind to do, Malcolm had, after his second trip to Africa, announced further plans to return to the continent in order to visit other African countries to make sure that his anti-American message was heard by more political leaders of Africa that he was yet to meet on the continent and at the UN, which he frequented.[5]

Due to Malcolm's anti-American propaganda overseas, U.S. officials and the security agencies tried to counteract his activities. That was why American officials chose to interview Alex Haley, who would later become well known for his Pulitzer Prize–winning book, *Roots*. Haley was collaborating with Malcolm on his autobiography, and the interview was to find out if he knew about any illegal acts of his friend. It was the time when it was merely confirmed that Malcolm X had unsuccessfully solicited the "support of the government of [President] Gamal Abdel Nasser for his activities on behalf of orthodox Islam in the United States."[6]

Haley, who was suspected by the U.S. officials of having knowledge of Malcolm X's foreign financial dealings, had become a pivotal figure in Malcolm's life since he wrote about the NOI leaders in an article published in the *Reader's Digest*. It was after Haley's March 1960 article about the NOI, which was titled "Mr. Muhammad Speaks" that the author and Malcolm X became close friends, a relationship that led to their collaboration on Malcolm's autobiography.[7] Haley was worried about the book project with Malcolm when Muhammad silenced his friend in December 1963; hence he traveled to Chicago to ascertain its implications from the NOI leader. Muhammad, who liked Haley very much for writing the positive *Readers' Digest* article about him and his NOI, assured Haley that the punishment was not going to be permanent.[8]

Meanwhile, in the fall of 1964, American officials stepped up their search into Malcolm's activities as the leader of MMI, Inc., and the OAAU. Ironically, the U.S. government's investigations of Malcolm's activities at this particular time were prompted by statements from other black American leaders who made inflammatory comments that fuelled the suspicions and actions of government investigators. A typical example was that then Student Nonviolent Coordinating Committee (SNCC) chairman John Lewis had allegedly bragged about Malcolm's overwhelming impact on the leaders of Africa. Lewis went on to add that he was personally aware of the fact that in every country that Malcolm visited in Africa, he was well received, and that the African leaders he met were receptive to Malcolm's anti-American comments. Also, it was confirmed by Manning Marable in his 2011 book that everywhere in Africa that Malcolm X visited, he "was treated like a visiting dignitary, and his prominence over the course of several days at social and public events must have stunned the CIA and the FBI."[9]

Possibly, American officials would not have been bothered if Malcolm simply concerned himself with improving relationships between African leaders and African Americans. What Malcolm did not realize was that, with Africa being one of the important growing Third World areas, every major nation at the time wanted to court the leaders of the second largest continent. That was why the U.S. Information Agency (USIA) director Carl Rowan, a black diplomat, tried his best to use his agency to minimize the havoc that Malcolm X was wreaking on American foreign policy. In discussions with African diplomats, Rowan, who was serving under the administration of President Lyndon B. Johnson, very carefully pointed to the 1964 Civil Rights Act as a positive step in the struggle for total equality for blacks and other minorities in America.[10]

Malcolm X, at this time in the fall of 1964, relished the idea that he was impacting American foreign policy with his actions on behalf of his fellow blacks, who were—in his opinion—being oppressed. USIA officials were armed with positive news releases about the United States for American journalists and their editors to use in counteracting negative reports about America locally and abroad by Malcolm X and others. Toward that end, the *New York Times* and other major news sources did disclose in published articles how American officials were taking further steps to counteract Malcolm X's global condemnation of the American government of the day. Matters were taken so seriously by American officials that the U.S. State Department as well as the Justice Department were jointly taking steps to address several aspects of Malcolm X's anti-American activities overseas and also at forums of international organizations. Part of the reasons for the lack of support for Malcolm X's propaganda was that the emergent independent African countries had social, political, and economic problems of their own. Furthermore, these black nations, as a bloc, were very much interested in such regional issues as the apartheid situation in South Africa, which was part of their continent, but not necessarily what was going on in America, which Malcolm was publicizing in negative ways. It was on this basis that African leaders bought into USIA Director Rowan's appeal to them to consider that the 1964 Civil Rights Act was a major improvement in the fortunes of blacks in America. Also, that was exactly what African leaders wanted to hear. Therefore, the leaders did not deem it necessary to issue a joint statement to condemn America in any way at the 1964 Organization of African Unity (OAU) annual conference in Cairo. Instead, to pacify Malcolm, his friends among a few of Africa's leaders in Cairo agreed to pass a mild, nonbinding resolution that urged the American government to devote some of its vast resources for fighting racism back in America, and that was how far they agreed to go to show a symbolic support for Malcolm.[11]

With all the intrigues about Malcolm X and claims of plots and counterplots against him in January 1965, one would think that efforts would have been made by the security authorities to offer him adequate protection. The suggestion for security measures for Malcolm X was due to the expressed safety concerns of his wife, Betty, after the February 14, 1965, firebombing of their home. Betty's vocal expression of concern about her husband's security did evoke a lot of empathy for the family of Malcolm X. Among other details, she was quoted by the news media and several writers as saying that the American police authorities and the press never took Malcolm seriously, even after the bombing of his family home. Betty lamented bitterly that nothing was being done in the context of personal security for her husband as a targeted Islamic leader and a public figure. This was especially so as a section of the security agencies and their leaders were even claiming that Malcolm might have committed the arson on his family home by himself to court sympathy as well as draw attention to his activities at the time. Since a court order confirmed that the home belonged to the NOI, which loaned it to Malcolm and his family, the suspicion of critics of Malcolm and his two organizations was that "Malcolm firebombed the house out of malice."[12]

Malcolm and his wife, Betty, had been told by their family physician that they were expecting twins and, as a result, they decided to turn their attention to find ways and means of supporting their growing family. Monetary matters would be worse because the arrival of the twins meant that Malcolm and Betty would have a total of six youngsters to feed, in addition to themselves. At the same time, Malcolm X had matters of his personal security to contend with. In fact, he was so much worried about his personal security that in mid-February 1965, he visited his Hotel Theresa headquarters to hold discussions with his leading associates of MMI and the OAAU, during which he complained bitterly that his staff was overemphasizing his problems with the NOI headquarters in Chicago. At that point, Malcolm's MMI, Inc., and OAAU colleagues, in unison, asked him to tell them where he thought his problems were coming, other than Chicago. Without mincing words, Malcolm X surprised them by forcefully telling them, "From Washington."[13]

Meanwhile, preparations were going on at this time for Malcolm to travel to Detroit to fulfill a speaking engagement. Since the firebombing of his house, Malcolm and his family were temporarily staying with friends in Queens, New York. Betty did not want him to travel out of town on the same day and leave them alone. Yet, Malcolm was not willing to cancel the event, which would also give him a speaking fee that he very much needed. According to eyewitness accounts, when Malcolm arrived in Detroit by plane and was picked up to be driven to the Statler Hotel, he still smelled of smoke from the firebombing incident at his home. Also, Malcolm complained of being tired from lack of sleep since the firebombing incident. For him to have a brief nap before his Detroit speaking engagement, a local friend gave Malcolm a sedative, but he had to wake up to be interviewed by WXYZ-Television that February 14, 1965, afternoon. After the interview, Malcolm was driven to the Ford Auditorium in central Detroit, where he delivered the keynote address at the first annual Dignity Projection and Scholarship Awards' event. At that event, the legendary actor Sidney Poitier and legendary singer Marian Anderson were scheduled to receive honors as well. The entire event was sponsored by the Afro-American Broadcasting Company, and local attorney Milton Henry, a very good friend of Malcolm X who was also an active member of the Michigan-based Freedom Now Party, chaired the event.[14]

The Reverend Albert Cleage of Detroit gave the invocation at the event, and at its conclusion that day, the local minister told OAAU and MMI, Inc., officials in discussions that Malcolm X seemed to be so tired that they should help him to go back to his hotel to rest. Since Malcolm also did complain to Rev. Cleage about smoke inhalation from the firebombing of his home, it was obvious that Malcolm X was said not to be as sharp a speaker as he was usually known to be. The audience was, however, thrilled by the fact that for the day's event, Malcolm decided to talk about his travels in the Middle East and Africa. In his speech, Malcolm told his audience proudly that the decade of 1955 to 1965 could be effectively described as the era during which the world would witness the emergence of Africa and its anticolonial freedom movement as well as the Non-Aligned Movement's Bandung conference spirit of Indonesia, where the movement held its maiden conference. During this period in the mid-1960s, the Non-Aligned Movement was headquartered in Indonesia, which was at the time under the leadership of President Sukarno, with whom Malcolm X had previously communicated. Sukarno's radical and pro-Non-Aligned Movement rhetoric had made it possible for oppressed Indonesians and other peoples of Southeast Asia to work hard for their own political freedom. This is similar to what Malcolm X saw in Africa on the part of colonial Africa's indigenous leaders, who had campaigned for the independence of their countries. Apart from using part of his speech to compare the U.S. civil rights movement with Africa's anticolonial movement, Malcolm touched on the year of 1965, during which he told his Detroit audience that what was confronting black men and women in America called for new methods, and that it would take power to talk to power, adding to the applause of the audience: "It takes madness almost to deal with a power structure that's so corrupt."[15]

Malcolm X was informed that when he was away in Detroit, officers of the New York Police Department (NYPD) visited the burned-out house from the firebombing, with the local news media also camped near there to get news about the firebombing. Meanwhile, NOI officials were angered by the fact that Malcolm X had not called them to report that the property that they were about to take from him and his family had suffered extensive damage through the firebomb. Later, the next day, on February 15, 1965, Malcolm returned from Detroit. That same evening, Malcolm's OAAU had planned a meeting for its members so that their leader would talk about the firebombing of his home. Given the circumstances, an event that was arranged to be small had turned into a large one, with not less than 700 OAAU members present. Malcolm used the opportunity to castigate the NOI and its leaders, including the tactics of trying to blame him for the firebombing of his home, with his family sleeping in it. While Benjamin X introduced the event with brief remarks, Malcolm decided to speak on the topic, "There is a Worldwide Revolution Going On."[16]

Although his ruined home had not totally been emptied of its burned-out and half-burned belongings, Malcolm had not gone back there to do so. Instead, he was traveling to fulfill speaking engagements, as that increased his visibility and gave him much-needed speaking fees. Therefore, upon returning from Detroit, Malcolm traveled to Rochester, New York, for a one-night trip, to give a speech. At the same time, local court records indicated that, by a judgment rendered in favor of Muhammad and his NOI, Malcolm and his family were to leave the firebombed house on February 18, 1965, so that the NOI officials would repossess the property, which was now burned out and ruined. Still, Malcolm knew that it was his responsibility to remove all the properties belonging to him and his family by the court-given deadline. To fulfill his promise to the court to abide by the ruling, Malcolm invited about a dozen MMI and OAAU members to join him very early in the morning of February 18, 1965, to assist with the clearing of his things from the house, basically in advance of the marshal's arrival with his employees. In about four hours, Malcolm and his helpers emptied the badly burned building of furniture, files, clothes, desks, historic photographs, and correspondence in files. He placed the salvageable personal items in four vehicles made up of a small van and three station wagons that they had on hand. Upon arrival on the premises to enforce the court order, the marshal and the employees from his department found the house completely empty.[17]

After the tedious task of going back to the destroyed house for the cleaning and salvaging of his remaining property, Malcolm felt so tired that he decided to contact the Mississippi Freedom Democratic Party leaders to reschedule an impending speaking engagement. However, after further consideration, he chose to give interviews that had been requested of him about the firebombing of his home. This was around February 19, 1965, barely two days before his assassination, and prophetically, Malcolm X, in an interview with the New York Times, told his interviewer that he was, at the time, living like a person already dead. That was one of several occasions on which Malcolm had made such comments in several weeks with reference to death, and with the firebombing of his home, observers felt that Malcolm was right about the possibility of death. He added that he expected violence and death to be part of the solution about his life. In fact, he repeated similar words when he appeared at Barnard College to address over 1,500 students. In addition to telling the students about his experiences from his trips overseas, particularly in Africa, Malcolm X underscored the rebellious nature of a world or global revolution against the oppressor, and ended the speech with his claim that, in America, the oppressor was "deliberately subjugating the Negro for economic reasons."[18]

When MMI and OAAU leaders, including Malcolm X, met to discuss the firebombing of their leader's family's residence, the resolution was that, as of that day, anybody attending events of their two organizations would be subjected to a search to make sure that there was safety for their leader, and indeed, for the audience in general. According to a spokesperson by the name of Peter Bailey, Malcolm disagreed with the searches, adding to the surprise of other leaders that security personnel of his organization should be unarmed at the scheduled Sunday, February 21, 1965 event in the Audubon Ballroom. He agreed to make an exception for his bodyguard and also his security chief, Reuben X

Francis, to be the only two armed that day. Since a young man by the name of Gene Roberts, a former naval officer, had allegedly been planted by the New York Police Department (NYPD) as a paid informant, he promptly informed his NYPD handlers or leaders about the insistence on Malcolm's part that, for the Sunday event, the security detail of the MMI, which was hosting the event, would be unarmed apart from the two designated to be armed. Manning Marable wrote in his 2011 biography of Malcolm X that Roberts "was the most important police operative inside the MMI and OAAU."[19] To prepare for the event, Malcolm decided to check into the New York Hilton Hotel, while his wife and the children stayed in their temporary home belonging to Tom Wallace. When some black people went to the hotel to ask about Malcolm X, the hotel's security personnel turned them away.[20]

According to Manning Marable in *A Life of Reinvention: Malcolm X*, the only reason that the pronounced death sentence had not been carried out was that Elijah Muhammad, as the NOI supreme leader, had not endorsed the decision. However, Marable added that given the convergence of interests between local law enforcement, American national security institutions, and the NOI, the murder of Malcolm X was becoming a realizable event. While things were becoming hectic for Malcolm, his wife, Betty, made it clear to him that she did not approve of Ms. Lynne Shifflett as the OAAU's secretary-general. Consequently, she resigned from that position, and Malcolm replaced her with Sara Mitchell. James X, as a member of the inner circles of Malcolm X, was relieved that Ms. Shifflett was no longer the secretary-general and, as a result, he promptly decided to have a better relationship with Ms. Mitchell, who was going to be in charge of the day-to-day activities of the OAAU, indeed to the delight of Betty, Malcolm's wife.[21]

For security reasons, Malcolm was still in a hideout, staying at the New York Hilton Hotel, as he planned to address a major OAAU event in the afternoon of February 21, 1965. Earlier in the week, he had urged his wife not to attend the scheduled OAAU event with their children for fear of violence taking place there. However, on the morning of February 21, Malcolm telephoned from the hotel to the home of the Wallaces, where his family was staying, to invite Betty to come with the children to attend the event. Although surprised, Betty was still happy about the invitation. Therefore, she began to dress the children at 1:00 P.M. for the late afternoon OAAU event. For their oldest child, Attallah Shabazz, it was exciting for the entire family to have the opportunity to go and see their father. Malcolm checked out of the hotel to attend the Audubon Ballroom event, driving his Oldsmobile, which he parked a few blocks away, and instead, got a ride in a vehicle being driven to the event by MMI member Charles X Blackwell. When they arrived at the ballroom, they did not see the usual security or police presence because of Malcolm's insistence that there should be no armed guards at the event, a situation that would make Malcolm's assassination easy to carry out by the plotters.[22]

It was on Sunday, February 21, 1965, exactly one week after his home was firebombed, that Malcolm X was shot to death. The NY Herald Tribune edition of Monday, February 22, 1965, had the bold headline of the assassination story written by Jimmy Breslin, its reporter at the OAAU event. His published story's headline was: "Malcolm X Slain by Gunmen as 400 in Ballroom Watch." The subheadline read: "Police Rescue Two Suspects." Those rescued were the suspected gunmen that Malcolm's guards wanted to beat to death, but were rescued by the local police. Present to watch such a sad and gruesome spectacle was Malcolm's family. As reported, he had just started to speak, beginning with the usual Islamic greeting of Asaalam Alekum, which was enthusiastically responded to by the OAAU audience. At that point, two men deliberately started to have a scuffle, which was designed to distract the attention of Malcolm's few guards. It was then that three men rushed toward Malcolm on the podium to start to shoot him at point black range with sawn-off guns, which wounded him mortally. The assailants escaped from the ballroom, pursued by several of Malcolm's supporters and guards. Police reports indicated that one of the three suspected gunmen was identified later as Talmadge Hayer, a 22-year-old resident of Paterson, New Jersey, who had also been shot in the leg by the time he got to the exit of the ballroom building. It was further alleged by the police that he had been wounded by Reuben Francis, a Malcolm guard, and that he was seized outside the building by several people pursuing him. A second suspect was also seized, and many persons from the crowd began to beat and kick Hayer as well as the second man. The third suspect escaped from the scene mainly because the crowd did not catch him in time. Hayer—who was mistakenly named Thomas Hayer in the records by the police—and the second man were saved because armed police officers showed up promptly after the assassination of Malcolm.[23]

The death of Malcolm, which shocked the public and the police alike, seemed inevitable but very much senseless. In answering questions about the assassination, several newspaper reporters went to seek credible answers from the New York court, where five eyewitnesses in the Audubon Ballroom testified in the Malcolm X assassination's pretrial that three men did the killing, and that the three were active black Muslims from the NOI, from which Malcolm seceded. The assassination was deemed so important by the news media that its investigation remained for several days on the front pages of the New York Times and in other national and international newspapers.[24]

Apart from preparations for large burial rites for Malcolm X, his supporters were also following the ongoing court arraignment of Talmadge ("Tommy") Hayer, Norman X Butler, and Thomas X Johnson, the three men charged with his murder. Lawyers for the suspects opposed their long detentions by the police, a matter that was raised in the New York Supreme Court, where application for bail was raised. New York Supreme Court Justice Abraham J. Gellinoff gave a pretrial ruling that the year-long detention of some of the Malcolm X assassination suspects, including Cary Thomas, was justified because they possessed much-needed "vital information concerning the identity of the perpetrators."[25]

The court trial of the three black men for capital murder, which lasted from January 12, 1966 to March 10, 1966, was presided over by Judge Charles Marks, with New York District Attorney Vincent Dermody leading the prosecution of the alleged assassins. On March 10, 1966, the trial's jury found all of the three defendants guilty in the first-degree assassination of Malcolm X. It had taken the racially mixed jury of nine men and three women more than 20 hours of posttrial deliberations to reach their verdict, which was announced to Judge Marks' court. The charge carried with it an automatic sentence of life in prison, with only the possibility of a parole after almost 27 years in jail for each convicted prisoner. The court did not buy the idea of conspiracy theorists, as quoted by the defense, that Malcolm X could have

Malcolm X's funeral, held on February 27, 1965, at the Faith Temple Church of God in Christ, in Harlem. (© Bob Adelman/Corbis)

been killed by the Central Intelligence Agency (CIA), the Federal Bureau of Investigations (FBI), or even international drug cartels.[26]

During the formal sentencing event, on April 14, 1966, the three accused persons—Hayer, Butler, and Johnson—stood convicted before Judge Marks. On that day, Defense Attorney Peter L. Sabbatino tried to discredit the verdict by telling the judge that he did not think that the verdict would be the required solution that history would support because, in his opinion, his clients were innocent. The judge did not accept the attorney's disputing argument. With the convicted assassins of Malcolm X standing very quiet and facing the bench, presiding judge Marks in a carefully-written sentencing remark announced that the three convicted black men were to be confined to state prison for the period of their natural lives, which meant a life sentence.[27]

Meanwhile, Washington attorney Edward Bennett Williams, who had been retained by friends for the accused persons, informed the court that he was going to file an appeal shortly after the verdict and sentencing of the convicted persons. The central issue at stake—in the defense attorney's legal opinion—was how a prosecution witness, by the simple abbreviated name of "Mr. T" (for fear of his life later) was allowed to testify in closed court instead of an open court. To the defense attorney, the closed court arrangement deprived the three accused persons the public trial the American constitution calls for in all capital murder cases. The defense attorney's appeal, filed on April 16, 1969, came before three empanelled New York Appeal Court judges, who were ready to hear the appeal, and subsequently, to rule on the defense attorney's objection to the closed court proceedings. The presiding judges of the court declared unanimously that in any trial that was otherwise open, a judge could use a discretion to close part of the trial during the testimony of a particular witness, especially if that was done for a good or a security reason that is directly related to the management of the trial. In that way, Judge Marks' decision, in Mr. T's testimony, did stand that test invoked by the defense attorney. Therefore, the assembled judges found no other reversible error in the 3,600–page trial record, and as a result, observed that the proof against all the three defendants was very much overwhelming or abundant. As a result, the three-panel judges unanimously confirmed that so far as the people of the State of New York were concerned, the Malcolm X case was closed, and that the three convicted black men should be returned to jail to begin to serve their life sentences.[28]

Although, the three convicted persons—Hayer, Butler and Johnson— went to jail to serve their sentences, defense Attorney Sabbatino further predicted that the trial would not be the end of the controversy, especially over who actually killed Malcolm X in the ballroom and, so far, that has been correct. For example, Hayer had confessed to his part of the crime, but the two other convicted persons did not. That is why some people, who supported Malcolm, still believed the conspiracy theories as being very much necessary to explain Malcolm's death in 1965 as well as Dr. King's death later in 1968. Both died under similar violent circumstances. Interestingly, both black leaders of America were, respectively, assassinated at age 39.

EPILOGUE: MALCOLM X'S LEGACY IN THE CONTEXT OF BLACK LEADERSHIP

Malcolm X used a wide range of philosophies, strategies, and tactics to make himself the complex individual that the United States celebrates today. His admirers have labeled him as a self-made man, and his critics have used the term "reinvented" to describe him. While it is difficult to find one word that accurately describes the totality of Malcolm X's personality and contributions, it is fair to say that his life included various aspects of self-metamorphosis that drew on the examples of black leaders from the past as well as inspiring black leaders of today.

In his life, Malcolm endured many unique changes, including those that affected his family circumstances, his education, and his lifestyle, as well as his religion and original name. The change in name was connected to his religious fervor, but it was also deeply rooted in the way of life of many of Malcolm's contemporaries. At the most basic level, the change in Malcolm X's name gave a hint of the dynamic life that he would eventually lead. For example, in Malcolm's 39 years of existence, there was a metamorphosis of his name, which had been changed on two separate occasions by the time he died on February 21, 1965. It was similar to the evolutionary processes that names of other black leaders underwent in the black diaspora and in Africa, the second largest continent of the world.

In the case of Malcolm—who was originally named Malcolm Little—he became "Malcolm X" in September 1952, when he first joined the Nation of Islam (NOI) to embrace the Islamic religion. He lived with his new name until 1964, barely a year before his untimely death, when Malcolm became El-Hajj Malik El-Shabazz. He attained the *El-Hajj* (or *Alhaji*) title on the basis of his Islamic pilgrimage (or Hajj) to Mecca with other Muslims. For the first time, Malcolm used the new name and title in a letter that he wrote from the Middle East to his loyal assistants back in the New York headquarters of the Muslim Mission, Incorporated (MMI), which he established after he left the NOI. Speaking of the varied transformations that he underwent in his short life, Malcolm observed in his co-authored and posthumously published autobiography that his "whole life had been a chronology of changes."[1]

Within the context of modern black history, the changes that society saw in Malcolm X were part of the fact that he was paradoxically either joining or helping to create a name-changing trend, as several black leaders—either in the United States or in African countries—were known to have done when they also changed their original names given to them at birth for a variety of reasons. The Reverend Martin Luther King, Jr., who was a few years younger than Malcolm, was named at birth in Atlanta, Georgia, as Michael Luther King, but he agreed for his original name to be changed to Martin Luther King, Jr., mainly for it to align with his namesake, the Reverend Martin Luther King, Sr., his father. Also, coming from a family of deeply seated Christian religious traditions and preachers, the Martin Luther portion was in honor of the famous German theologian and Protestant hero, Martin Luther. Another American black leader who changed his name was Stokely Carmichael, who succeeded John Lewis in 1966 as president of the U.S.-based radical Student Nonviolent Coordinating Committee (SNCC). In view of his strong belief in pan-Africanism, Carmichael changed his name in 1969 to Kwame Ture, in honor of Ghana's former president Kwame Nkrumah and Guinea's late president SekouToure. Under very similar pan-African and Islamic circumstances, the heavyweight boxing champion, Muhammad Ali, was born Cassius Clay, but upon embracing the Honorable Elijah Muhammad's NOI, he had his name changed, with the first part of Muhammad being in honor of the NOI leader.[2]

Africa, which Malcolm X visited enthusiastically, seemed to be the origin for the name-changing trend that Malcolm X and other future black leaders embraced in the United States, as the practice was a known phenomenon among several of the anticolonial nationalist black leaders that Malcolm met when he visited the African continent between 1964 and 1965. They included Nigerian president Nnamdi Azikiwe, who was named Benjamin Azikiwe at birth. However, he angrily changed his name to his indigenous one in the 1930s, when he was, as a top athlete, not permitted by British colonial officials to run in London's Empire Games (now called British Commonwealth Games) because his country had not attained independence. Kenyan president Jomo Kenyatta, whom Malcolm X met in 1964 in the East African nation's capital of Nairobi, was named Kamauwa Ngengi at birth on October 20, 1893, in Gatundu, Kenya, but when studying social anthropology at the London School of Economics (LSE) in the 1930s, he decided to change his original name to that of Jomo Kenyatta to reflect his anti-British colonialist and nationalist aspirations. Also, Ghanaian president Kwame Nkrumah was named Francis Nwia-Kofi Nkrumah at birth in 1909 in the Gold Coast (now called the Republic of Ghana). Upon completing his undergraduate and graduate studies at Pennsylvania-based Lincoln University and the University of Pennsylvania, respectively, Nkrumah changed his name to Kwame Nkrumah, thereby no longer making use of his first two original names of Francis Nwia.[3]

To a large extent, Malcolm X was correct in his assertion that his life had been a chronology of changes. After all, he went through many changes in order to be recognized as a true Muslim and eventually as an Islamic leader. The formidable changes Malcolm underwent included learning from his two brothers how to comport himself, showing respect for black leadership, and accepting the teachings of the Honorable Elijah Muhammad as NOI leader, who was known as the messenger or apostle of God (or Allah, as the Muslims called God). To Malcolm's delight, those teachings included the way his original name was to change from Malcolm Little to reflect an Islamic name upon becoming a Muslim one day, as he already saw his surname of Little as a slave name. The changes that Malcolm underwent also affected what he ate or consumed, as his two brothers (an older brother and a younger brother) taught him, when still in prison, that he was not to eat pork, not to smoke, and not to talk in a certain crude way. Apart from considerable reading in prison about the way enslaved blacks were arbitrarily given names by their slave masters, Malcolm also saw a name change as part of the Islamic practice. Therefore, when he was to join the NOI, he had to follow the instructions he had received from several experienced Muslims. Such instructions included advice from his two brothers about the importance of a name change, drawing on a Chinese analogy that Muhammad taught his followers and his fellow NOI leaders. Muhammad—whose birth name was Elijah Poole—had asserted that it would be ridiculous for a Chinese person to appear before black people to announce that his name was, for example, Patrick Murphy, Patrick O'Brien, or Patrick Kennedy—all typical Irish names. In that way, it was clear that, as Malcolm Little, the future Muslim convert carried an Anglicized name when he was given that name at birth.[4]

MALCOLM X'S ULTIMATE CONTROVERSY IN DEATH IN 1965

Malcolm X was considered by many people to be a controversial figure in life and also in death. The controversy included the fact that although many people mourned his death in 1965, others did not want to be associated with him. That is why, even in death, Malcolm X needed the assistance of attorney Percy Sutton to help select his final resting place. Sutton was a pioneering black legal figure who represented Malcolm X when he was alive as well as when he died in 1965. His family circumstances were similar to those of Malcolm X, his client. For example, while Malcolm inherited his oratorical skills from his Baptist-preaching father, Sutton also acquired his passion for higher education and civil rights from his own father, Mr. Samuel Johnson Sutton. Upon receiving a decent education like Malcolm's father, Sutton's father chose to become the principal of a segregated high school in San Antonio, Texas, while his mother Lillian was a teacher and mother of 15 children. Her educational background was similar to that of Malcolm's Caribbean-born mother, Mrs. Louise Little.[5]

Like other paradoxes surrounding Malcolm's life, Percy Sutton was first invited, by chance, to go and listen to a wonderful black speaker by the name of Malcolm X, who was scheduled to give a lecture at 125th Street and Seventh Avenue in Harlem. It was at this event that the young Sutton introduced himself to Malcolm X as a local attorney, and he later agreed to assist Malcolm with some specific legal matters and, at Malcolm's request, to serve as his lawyer from that time forward. Certainly, Malcolm, as a black Muslim leader at the time, very desperately needed a trained lawyer to handle various legal matters in which he was involved, including the drafts of contracts for the publication of his impending autobiography, which he was discussing with various publishing companies. Therefore, Sutton was often invited to represent Malcolm X whenever he needed legal help and, after his assassination in 1965, when cemeteries in the New York area refused to sell a burial plot for Malcolm's internment. Apart from racism being seen by Malcolm X's followers as part of the real problem in finding a local cemetery to bury their leader, it was also a fact that there was genuine concern that any place used to bury such a controversial Muslim leader could easily suffer desecration by white supremacist groups like the Ku Klux Klan (or KKK). Therefore, it became necessary for Sutton to arrange for Malcolm to be buried out of town, in New York's Westchester County. During the burial ceremony, something interesting happened. Since the cemetery's grave workers were all white men, Malcolm's friends from his MMI and Organization of Afro-American Unity (OAAU) decided that before they left the burial grounds, they should be given shovels so that "under a drizzling rain, the brothers proceeded to bury Malcolm themselves."[6]

MALCOLM AS AN INTERNATIONAL FIGURE

Malcolm X's dynamic personality and his interest in the international dimensions of nationalist black politics were important in the organizational and recruitment apparatuses of black social, cultural, and political organizations. To attain his objective of being able to interact successfully with some of the leaders he met overseas, particularly in the Middle East and Africa, Malcolm X needed trusted friends in terms of contacts from men and women in both areas. Some of these men and women received Malcolm X warmly. Furthermore, these leaders made serious and concerted efforts to contact Malcolm on a regular basis. For example, letters in Malcolm X's records at the Harlem-based Schomburg Center for Research in Black Culture showed that in the winter of 1964, an African American scholar by the name of Julian Mayfield, who had met Malcolm back in Ghana, wrote to Malcolm from the West African nation with the sole aim of suggesting the establishment of an organization of some sort that would have institutional links to the African American community in the Western Hemisphere. It was also expected to connect the African American expatriate community in Africa and the Ethiopia-based young organization known as the Organization for African Unity (OAU), which was established by African leaders in 1963 to spearhead efforts for continental unity. Subsequently, Mayfield, who was an African American writer living in the Ghanaian capital of Accra, offered to represent on the African continent any new organizations that Malcolm founded.

Although Malcolm X's overseas trips included his political and social interests, he took the time to make it known publicly that the journeys outside of the United States were primarily for religious reasons. For example, in the Middle East, Malcolm went on the Islamic pilgrimage (or Hajj) to Mecca for him to live up to his lifelong quests and interests as a Muslim. In his opinion, such a trip would increase and deepen his knowledge of the Islamic religion. That was a crucial goal because Malcolm was then in conflict with the Honorable Elijah Muhammad and his NOI leaders. After all, it was widely known that Malcolm's credibility rested on his religious affiliations.

Malcolm X placed great importance on going to Ghana, which was the first British colony in sub-Saharan Africa to attain independence on March 6, 1957. Malcolm felt very comfortable with the fact that several African American compatriots of his, who chose to leave the United States to go and live in Africa, decided to go to West African countries, including Ghana. Such emigrating African American leaders included the legendary Dr. W. E. B. Du Bois, who died there in 1963, as well as his wife, Shirley, who continued to live in Ghana up to the time that Malcolm visited the country. Interestingly, Malcolm knew that Dr. Du Bois and his wife renounced their American citizenship in order to become naturalized Ghanaian citizens, which was after several years of being intimidated and labeled as either social-ists or even communists by American security agencies, including the Federal Bureau of Investigation (FBI). Therefore, Dr. and Mrs. Du Bois as well as Maya Angelou, St. Claire Drake, and other African Ameri-can intellectuals went to Ghana and other African countries to fulfill personal pilgrimages of their own. African Americans who chose to go to Ghana were responding to invitations extended by the new leader of the country's decolonization struggle. For example, Malcolm X and other U.S.-based black leaders still recalled how, in 1954 at a Lincoln University commencement, then prime minister Kwame Nkrumah el-oquently appealed to Western democracies and black men and women to return to Africa to help Ghana and other nations on the continent to assist development programs that were taking place in newly inde-pendent African countries.[7]

Being among the top black leaders of the civil rights era in the United States, Dr. Martin Luther King, Jr., and Malcolm X had, separately and on different occasions, visited and held detailed discussions with Nkrumah and several of Ghana's new leaders (in 1957 and 1964, respec-tively). Nkrumah was very comfortable in holding mutual discussions with the two black leaders from the United States, but it was ironic that Malcolm and King, who had met Nkrumah, were later assassinated in similar circumstances back in the United States. Nkrumah reportedly expressed shock when both black leaders were killed. Nkrumah had his own government subsequently overthrown in a combined plot of mili-tary and police officers in a foreign-inspired coup d'état on February 24, 1966. The overthrow of Nkrumah's government in Ghana forced him to flee into exile to live in President Sekou Toure's Guinea, during which Nkrumah died from cancer in April 1972.

Malcolm X, Stokely Carmichael, and other U.S.-based black lead-ers, who changed their names and also frequented African countries to interact with their leaders, gained ideologically and otherwise. For example, they were unabashedly and fearlessly able to interact with socialist diplomatic missions at the United Nations. In the midst of the Cold War that was going on worldwide between the socialist East and the capitalist West, many scholars wondered if Malcolm X was not en-dangering himself, as an American citizen, by showing a fascination for or an infatuation with foreign ideologies. At the time, it was obvious that Malcolm X had met socialist leaders of Africa, for whom he had admiration, and that he also admired the Chinese revolution led by Mao Zedong. Malcolm X went to the extent of directly calling on the Chinese leaders and their Communist Party to take a public stance in support of the ongoing African American civil rights struggles by the various organizations within the movement. Chairman Mao issued a public statement in the early1960s in support of the civil rights struggle in the United States, in which, among other details, he wrote that the black struggle was not only a struggle waged by the exploited and oppressed black people for freedom and emancipation, but that it was also a new loud call on all of the exploited and oppressed men and women of the United States to fight against their oppression. Malcolm did not visit China or Cuba, but the socialist environments he most admired drew its examples from the models of Chairman Mao and Cuba's Castro.[8]

Apart from being suspected to be anti-establishment and an Islamic saboteur by FBI director J. Edgar Hoover and other national security experts of the National Security Agency (NSA), Malcolm X had an infatuation with socialist ideas, most of which were unpopular during the anti-communist witchhunt of the McCarthy era. At that time, socialists and communists were being treated alike as public enemies. Yet, those who knew Malcolm very well within Muslim circles held the strong opinion that he did not see socialism as a viable alternative to capitalism in America. Instead, he wanted to be seen as a good Muslim, who happened to have extensive local and international friends of all political persuasions. For example, contrary to the suspicion of American security leaders like Hoover and others, it was not because Malcolm was simply rich for him to endeavor to plan a journey to Mecca to perform the traditional Muslim pilgrimage. Instead, he was merely subscribing to the prevailing notion that every good Muslim must do so at least once in a lifetime. After all, his former NOI leader and mentor, the Honorable Elijah Muhammad, had also visited Mecca for his own pilgrimage. At the same time, for an entire month, Muhammad, accompanied by members of his family, took the time to visit several places in Africa and in the Middle East between November and December 1959, indeed about five years before Malcolm embarked on his own pilgrimage foray into the Middle East and Africa.[9]

Malcolm X had opportunities to embark on a lot more travels abroad than Muhammad. Furthermore, Malcolm's own very extensive travels took place later between April 1964 and early spring of 1965—journeys that shaped the latter part of his life as well as his overall thought process. In Islamic religious circles in the United States as well as in black politics, Malcolm X's name became a household word for young and old blacks alike. Indeed, Malcolm's carefully orchestrated and detailed overseas travels, about which he later lectured, eventually became very important in understanding as well as defining the totality of Malcolm's being.

MALCOLM AS AN ICONIC FIGURE

Malcolm X's life came to an abrupt end on that fateful Sunday of February 21, 1965, when he was shot to death in the presence of his wife and children. Yet, several commentators and writers—including Manning Marable—have pointed out without equivocation that Malcolm X has, in our time, acquired iconic status in the pantheon of multicultural American heroes. When alive, he supposedly exhibited strength and the ability to adapt to new situations, the performance that Marable described as his "reinvention." Malcolm X—who met Dr. King on only one occasion on March 26, 1964, in the U.S. Capitol in Washington, D.C.—was in leadership terms and in intensity for black freedom in America very much like King, the Nobel Peace Prize–winning black civil rights leader. King was also described by his admirers and independent analysts as having a similar great gift, which was his powerful ability to speak. Malcolm's oldest daughter, Attallah Shabazz, has described Malcolm as a lover of language, who "very much believed in the power of words to influence as well as to transform human lives."[10]

In the end, Malcolm X has come to occupy a very central space in the folk tradition of what commentators and other observers saw as the realm of black outlaws and dissidents. Yet, in the afterword that he wrote for the 1999 reissued edition of Malcolm X's autobiography, Ossie Davis pointed out that by snatching Malcolm X away, death had created an irreplaceable void of the black leader who transformed himself shortly before his assassination. To Davis, no person who happened to know

Malcolm X before and after his pilgrimage to Mecca "would doubt that he had completely abandoned racism, separatism, and hatred."[11]

Davis summed up Malcolm X's life without fear or favor in the same afterword. Without hesitation, he pointed out all of Malcolm's traits—including warts and all—indeed, many details that his admirers and family members had wished were forgotten. Yet, Davis pointed out that for many years in Malcolm X's life, he was known to have been a criminal as well as an addict and, indeed, "a pimp, and a prisoner, a racist, and a hater, [who] had really believed the white man was a devil. But all this has changed."[12]

Manning Marable, in his biography of Malcolm X, described such changes in the person of the assassinated black Muslim leader as "a reinvention." That, in itself, was a reaffirmation of Malcolm's own words when he described the change in his life in one of his last interviews with Gordon Parks for *Life* magazine. In the interview, Malcolm looked back at his life with candor and, just as Davis described it in his own afterword to his autobiography, the OAAU leader said to his interviewer that his past was, in fact, behind him. He even regretted the way that he answered a white girl who wanted to help in bridging the racial divide, when Malcolm "refused her desire to volunteer her services to his association, causing her to burst into tears."[13] Like his contemporary, Martin Luther King, Jr., as a civil rights activist, Malcolm X felt the need to shoulder part of the burden of black people of America, including their struggles for human dignity and civil rights. Apart from being close in age, Malcolm X and King seemed to share similar views about life and death. It was obvious that Malcolm X and King, as public figures and civil rights activists, did not want to shy away from the possibility of being assassinated. Barely 24 hours before his own assassination in Memphis, Tennessee, on April 4, 1968, Dr. King gave his prophetic "I Have Been to the Mountain Top" speech, in which he boldly told his audience that he was not afraid of death. Similarly, Malcolm demonstrated his own fearless attitude toward death when he asked his security agents not to bring guns or arms to the February 21, 1965, event, during which he would be assassinated.[14]

Both of their widows took some comfort in the fact that their murdered husbands were not afraid of dying for the causes in which they believed. While Mrs. King went on to continue Dr. King's civil rights work through the Atlanta-based Martin Luther King, Jr. Center for Nonviolent Social Change, Dr. Betty Shabazz also did much to honor the memory of her late husband. In the case of Betty, several commentators have concluded that, like Mrs. King, she lived a successful life. After making sure that her children were old enough to concentrate on their education, Betty, in 1972, enrolled in a doctoral program at the University of Massachusetts in Amherst, where she received her doctoral (Ed.D.) degree in 1975, with which she became an administrator at Medgar Evers College in Brooklyn, the institution that had been named in honor of Mississippi-born Medgar Evers, the National Association for the Advancement of Colored People's field secretary who was shot to death outside his home in Jackson, Mississippi, by a sniper.[15]

In spite of the successes that Betty had achieved in the area of higher education and public recognition, tragedy still seemed to haunt the Shabazz clan. On June 23, 1997, Betty Shabazz died from her burn wounds when her troubled 12-year-old grandson by the name of Malcolm Shabazz allegedly set her home ablaze. The youngster was reportedly trying to find a way to force his grandmother to allow him to move back to his mother's home. When she died from the burns sustained in the fire, several public figures made favorable comments about Malcolm X's widow after her tragic death. In a public statement, then president Bill Clinton applauded her for her public commitments to education as well as her hard work in promoting the well-being of women and children. Also, District of Columbia House Representative Eleanor Holmes Norton pointed out that Betty was like her late husband, Malcolm, because she would be remembered not just for her death "but for the principled life she lived and the tower of strength she became."[16]

As if the family of Malcolm X had not already seen its own share of tragedy, on May 10, 2013, Malcolm Shabazz was killed in a night club assault in Mexico City. The Shabazz family was united in grief and, as a result, a consoling statement was issued to mourn young Malcolm's violent death in Mexico, which was reminiscent of the deaths of his great grandfather Earl Little and grandfather Malcolm X. In the family statement, it read, in part, that Malcolm Shabazz, in death, "now rests in peace in the arms of his grandparents and the safety of God."[17]

In spite of the fact that the deaths of Malcolm X, his father, and his grandson have been attributed to violence, the United States and the world at large still remember Malcolm X as the black Muslim revolutionary leader who died in 1965 after he had reinvented his life to become a respectable national icon worthy of high honor. Malcolm's importance has also prompted the naming in his honor of several places, including schools and streets both in United States and outside its borders.

THE OVERALL IMPACT OF MALCOLM X ON ORGANIZATIONS, SOCIETY, AND INDIVIDUALS

Perhaps one of the most contemporary black leaders to claim an affinity with Malcolm X is Clarence Thomas, the Supreme Court Justice who benefitted from the nomination of President George H. W. Bush on July 1, 1991. Justice Thomas, who succeeded the first black Supreme Court Justice Thurgood Marshall, to the surprise of several of his fellow blacks, has said unabashedly that Malcolm X was one of his heroes. In fact, he went on to point out that black liberals should not claim Malcolm X as their own because the assassinated Islamic leader and civil rights activist would never have gone to the Labor Department begging for a job or a handout. As a college student, Thomas insisted that Malcolm X's focus on self-sufficiency and black self-reliance were fundamental to his success. To the justice, Malcolm X's black or minority nationalist philosophy meant that black people should find freedom in hard work and determination rather than on the basis of affirmative action, integration, or other race-based remedies. Justice Thomas has further claimed that those sentiments were not only evident in Malcolm X's beliefs, but also in the philosophical underpinning of Thomas's own grandfather, who raised him, about whom he wrote eloquently in his published memoirs, titled My Grandfather's Son: A Memoir. Also, in a 2010 Supreme Court case on gun control, Justice Thomas based his support for gun rights on the historical importance of guns in holding back the violence of the Ku Klux Klan, White Knights, Pale Face Society, and others in the early 20th century. His defense of gun rights was very similar to Malcolm X's claims that black people should achieve freedom "by any means necessary."[18]

In assessing Malcolm X's overall impact, several black commentators have looked at Justice Thomas's references to him, and also wondered whether or not the black Muslim radical by the name of Malcolm X was, in fact, a black conservative in disguise. To a large extent, Malcolm X embraced certain tenets of conservatism with reference to religion, morals, self-reliance, and a disdain for forced integration. Many of these are underlying tenets of the Republican Party, even though the disdain for racial integration is not a tolerated public sentiment today. Still, the disdain is shown by the racially segregated neighborhoods and schools that define much of contemporary American life, even in our day. However, Malcolm X's focus on separation (rather than either segregation or forced integration) goes a long way to undermine the suggestion by some conservatives that, given some of his views, Malcolm was a thoroughgoing conservative. That is because his focus on separation focused on the ability of blacks to control their own destinies and reliance on themselves for progress and advancement. Today's black conservatives, however, are often the products of predominantly white institutions, but not outright separate institutions, including historically black colleges or black-owned businesses. Such is the limit of overlaying a conservative ideology on Malcolm X. While it is safe to say that he shared certain social and moral beliefs that are rooted in conservatism and the Islamic religion, they did not extend wholly to Malcolm X's political and economic agenda.

MALCOLM X'S AUTOBIOGRAPHY: ITS EVOLUTION AND IMPACT

The Autobiography of Malcolm X is considered a classic on college campuses all over the country and even throughout the wide world outside of the United States. It provides a deeper treatment of African American leadership than is usually allowed by the traditional focus on slavery and the Reverend Martin Luther King, Jr. The book was the basis for Spike Lee's 1992 film, *Malcolm X*, which was shown in thousands of theaters across the United States. Several leaders of high schools brought teachers and students to the theaters in their various neighborhoods to watch the film as part of their history and civic lessons. Some organizations like the Boys and Girls Clubs in

Los Angeles benefitted from a preview of the movie when their leaders and selected members were invited to watch and to provide their comments. The film reenergized interest in Malcolm X's autobiography. It showed Malcolm X as a social gadfly, whose willingness to dissent from the normal decorum of his day as well as to open his mouth too widely to critique the governmental establishment was detested by the security chiefs, including FBI director Hoover. Furthermore, his supporters harbored the feeling that Malcolm's antigovernment statements could have played a part in his assassination, although his admirers still hold the opinion that Malcolm's critical views of racism and injustice made for the betterment of American society. In one sense, the autobiography, which in turn, inspired the movie, revitalized black consciousness among inner-city youth in the early 1990s. It continues to teach the young men and women of today's society that Malcolm X was uncompromising about the evils of racism and the importance of self-reliance. Yet, the reinvention of his life, from a petty criminal and a felon to a revolutionary black leader worthy of posthumous respect and honor in our day, serves as a manifesto for other young black men and women, who have always yearned for a more meaningful life than what they are faced with.

Invariably, the autobiography has meant different things to different people. For example, in an eloquent foreword to the 1999 edition of *The Autobiography of Malcolm X*, Atallah Shabazz, the oldest of the six daughters of Malcolm and Betty, confirmed the fact that over 10 million people have come to know her late parents through their reading of the publication. Among other details, Atallah added the following memorable words to the foreword: "*The Autobiography of Malcolm X* has served as an everlasting testament to my father's life and legacy."[19]

It is also in Ms. Shabazz's foreword that she has confirmed her relationship as god child to Alex Haley, the collaborating co-author of the book. The context was couched in the following words, whereby she wrote that, given the circumstances of the 1960s, when the book was being published, "both my father and my godfather, Alex Haley, should feel a lot of peace to know that in the 'Best Issue of the Century' edition of *Time Magazine*, the autobiography was named as one of the top ten works of nonfiction of this century."[20]

*Dr. Betty Little Shabazz,
the widow of Malcolm X,
holding a copy of her late
husband's autobiography.
(© Rick Maiman/Sygma/
Corbis)*

Malcolm X's autobiography was published under circumstances
that were very much similar to the posthumous publication of Martin
Luther King's own autobiography, both of which needed literary editors to shepherd them through successful publication. For example, the
King scholar Clayborne Carson of Stanford University collaborated in
the capacity as an editor in putting together several autobiographical
notes that eventually constituted the volume that was posthumously
published in 1998, under the title *The Autobiography of Martin Luther
King, Jr.* With Malcolm's autobiography being similarly published posthumously in early 1965, Alex Haley helped in putting together the
manuscript through a series of in-depth interviews that the journalist conducted with Malcolm between 1963 and 1965. According to
various commentators and academic reviewers, Malcolm X's autobiography, to a large extent, underscores the militant black Muslim's philosophy of pan-Africanism as well as black nationalism and, indeed, black
pride. Although the main manuscript for the book was basically ready
to go to press when Malcolm X was assassinated in 1965, Haley took

the time to write his detailed epilogue to the published book, in which he informed his readers how the book came to be written and, also, to provide an overview of Malcolm X's impression of several black leaders and professionals. In fact, it was in the epilogue that Haley disclosed that, from several conversations that Malcolm had with him on various occasions, he "deduced that he [Malcolm] actually had a reluctant admiration for Dr. King."[21]

Haley also wrote in the epilogue that Malcolm X showed a lot of anger due to some comments made about black Muslims by Justice Marshall when he was still the staff attorney for the National Association for the Advancement of Colored People (NAACP). Specifically, Haley revealed in the epilogue that what angered Malcolm was Marshall's statement to the effect that the Muslims, in his opinion, were being run by thugs, who organized the group "from prisons and jails and financed, I am sure, by some Arab group."[22]

Initially, Haley's role in producing the autobiography was considered controversial, as to whether he was a ghostwriter or simply a collaborator. Today, literary commentators, in seeing the extensive nature of Malcolm X's activities overseas and also in the United States incorporated in the autobiography, have come to agree that Haley was simply a collaborator with Malcolm X but not the only force behind the autobiography. Malcolm's collaboration on the book was deemed very significant. For example, when it was published after his death in 1965, several prominent newspapers, magazines, and scholars reviewed the book. The *New York Times*, for example, described the autobiography as being brilliant as well as painful but, above all, an important book. Then, based on a screenplay adaptation by celebrated black writer James Baldwin and Arnold Perl, a play was developed that was so well received that it eventually provided the source for most of what New York–based film director Spike Lee relied on to produce his 1992 film, *Malcolm X*. The screenplay was developed by Baldwin into a full-fledged 1972 book titled, *One Day, When I Was Lost: A Scenario*, which was based strictly on the reinterpretation of *The Autobiography of Malcolm X*.

Several aspects of the autobiography of Malcolm X go a long way to demonstrate how black men and women become embittered in American society. For example, as a youngster, Malcolm learned about the death of his father happening under shady and violent circumstances.

His mother was also basically forced to enter a mental asylum when she was deemed incapable of taking care of her many children after her husband, Earl, died mysteriously. As Malcolm painfully saw and documented in his published memoirs, he and his siblings were spread across the state in foster homes. The autobiographical information on Malcolm X has been presented by Malcolm and his co-author (Haley) in several interesting ways to help readers understand and appreciate it. For example, 1925–1945 dealt with his birth and formative years, but 1946–1952 entailed his sordid years of crime, imprisonment of about a decade, of which not less than six years were to be served in prison environment. It was during this time, as clearly discussed in the auto-biography, that Malcolm went through various metamorphoses. In a variety of ways, Malcolm deserved commendation in showing, through his published memoirs, that if he could be rescued and saved from his many faults, then other young Americans—black and white alike—should not feel perpetually lost.

Malcolm X's example of coming from a poor background to become an icon prompted the Reverend Jesse Jackson and other black leaders to invoke the "I am somebody" slogan of the 1970s, several years after the black Muslim leader's assassination. Jackson was of the opinion that when a person is born in an American ghetto or slum area, he should shake off the ghetto (or slum) epithet in order to move forward in his or her life. As an ordained minister, he often preached that it was similar to when a dog, in labor, desperately enters an unlit oven to give birth. Just because they were born in an oven does not mean the dog's puppies should be called biscuits. In this sense, Malcolm was born in the midst of dire circumstances, but he was able to move beyond those circumstances to contribute in powerful and very useful ways to American life. It is impressive that Malcolm X still succeeded in becoming an iconic figure—what Manning Marable and other writers have described as a model of black encouragement and success. In a very real sense, Malcolm's success would pave the way for the successful mayoral victory of Harold Washington in Chicago in 1983; in the unusually strong voter turnouts in black neighborhoods when Jackson ran for president in 1984 and 1988; and of course, in the successful presidential electoral victories of President Barack Obama in today's generation. From his utterances, Malcolm X predicted that the votes of his fellow blacks would, in the end, change the balance of power in future electoral victories, just as was seen in the 2008 and 2012 presidential elections in the United States.

It was not until the publication of Malcolm's autobiography that he could be viewed as a true intellectual, as the published book provided valuable information in the study of black history in general, and African American history in particular. Therefore, as of 1965, when the autobiography was published, scholars, students, and ordinary readers— who had not taken the time to read it in much detail—had good reason to regard it as an outline for the author's philosophy of black nationalism as well as black pride and, possibly, pan-Africanism. Such black writers and scholars as professors Arnold Rampersad and Eric Dyson, a biographer of Malcolm X, have since concluded that one could see in the book aspects of what they have described as St. Augustine's confessional approach. Such reevaluations helped to minimize the depiction of Malcolm, in life and in death, as a mere black Muslim agitator, a racial extremist, and as a messiah of hate. Apart from individuals heaping those epithets on Malcolm X, the U.S. media, in the words of New York–based Union Theological Seminary professor James E. Cone, did unleash its venom against Malcolm although, in his opinion, both King and Malcolm X should be seen as being important "because they symbolize two necessary ingredients in the African-American struggle for justice in the United States."[23]

Surprisingly, several national newspapers, too, severely criticized Malcolm X through their postassassination reporting and editorial commentaries. For example, the *Washington Post* went to the extent of describing Malcolm as being a spokesman of bitter racism. At the same time, the *New York Times* described him as an irresponsible demagogue. Some of the newspapers as well as radio and television announcers predicted that Malcolm X could be replaced, after his assassination, by what they described as more virulent extremists. On the other hand, scholars and commentators have come to see Malcolm X very clearly through the lens of his autobiography. Malcolm X's involvement in the project has a history of its own. Initially, there were two articles that Alex Haley wrote about Muhammad as the NOI leader and also about Malcolm X in *Reader's Digest* and in *Playboy Magazine*, respectively. It has, however, been confirmed in available research sources that what brought the two black men closer were two events after their first meeting in 1959—the first being when Malcolm X named Haley as the godfather of his first child, Atallah; and then, in 1963, Doubleday Publishing Company asking Haley to write a book manuscript about Malcolm X for publication. The project eventually became the autobiography, which was started with the permission of Muhammad, as Malcolm was still with the NOI at the time.[24]

With Malcolm X's large family at home, it was agreed upon between himself and Haley that they needed a quieter place to begin work on the autobiography, which required several hours of interviewing sessions each day. Although Malcolm did not appreciate certain facts about Haley, he decided to make things work well between them if the project was to succeed. For example, Malcolm was unhappy about the Christian heritage of Haley as well as his middle-class status, and the fact that he had served in the U.S. Coast Guard, which is a branch of the U.S. Armed Forces. Eventually, Haley and Malcolm settled on a writing studio in New York's Greenwich Village, not far from New York University. There, they began interviewing sessions for between two hours and three hours each day. Haley helped Malcolm to focus on the relevant details for the book, instead of always trying to speak in praise of Muhammad. The interviews for the book went very well when Haley started to ask him about Malcolm's parental heritage, especially his mother and other family members.[25]

Although some critics have often made it seem that Haley was essentially the ghostwriter for Malcolm X, certain details suggest otherwise. For example, Haley did have unlimited control over the literary expressions and contents of the book. In the epilogue to the book, for example, Haley described an agreement he had with Malcolm X in order to allow his collaboration. Toward that end, Malcolm arrogantly told Haley that nothing could be in the autobiography that he did not say, and also that nothing could be left out without his permission. Part of their written agreement was that upon the conclusion of the main chapters for the autobiography, in a manuscript format, Haley would have the opportunity to add his own written comments at the end in the form of an epilogue, which was not to be read by Malcolm X. Since Malcolm was not to censor what Haley was going to add to the manuscript on his own, it did not make any difference that Haley's comments in the epilogue were being compiled for inclusion in the book after Malcolm was assassinated, before the autobiography's publication. As it has been shown over the years, the collaboration on the autobiography between Malcolm X and Haley was not the usual narrator and editor relationship. Instead, it was for Haley to listen to Malcolm X and, in the process, capture the essentials to compose and include in the manuscript. Of course, it has been demonstrated that Malcolm X did dominate the ongoing autobiographer–biographer relationship when he worked with Haley. Although Haley has described in his epilogue how he edited the manuscript, he made it obvious that Malcolm essentially controlled the language used to craft the chapters. Once trust was established, Malcolm never hesitated to tell Haley some of the "most intimate details of his personal life, over the next two years."[26]

Malcolm's autobiography details several aspects of his life toward the end of his imprisonment and upon becoming a Muslim. For example, due to the teachings of the NOI that came through his two siblings in the NOI, Malcolm gave up gambling as well as smoking and crime. Yet, several reviewers of the autobiography have shown in their reviews that Malcolm's experiences as an evangelist after his imprisonment invariably did look like his years of being a hustler. Furthermore, Malcolm endeavored to make the published autobiography evoke laughter by adding some specific details, including the fact that he told his campus audiences that the students went to college for four years or more to earn academic degrees but that, on his part, he earned his bachelor's degree from the streets of Harlem, New York. What was also apparent at the time, as narrated by Malcolm and incorporated in his autobiography, was that he did not leave out some unpleasant details, including the hustling experiences he survived, which were however not part of the experiences that he needed to succeed in his future role in the NOI. Yet, he candidly wrote about all of them, as it seemed that all experiences on his part were useful. Readers could see how some of Malcolm X's street experiences were unpleasant, as they included trading in illegal drugs to make money to survive. However, as he recounted in his autobiography, as a hustler, he often returned to the streets of Harlem to be with other hustlers, but he was no longer useful as a hustler after he embraced Islam. The main reason was that, as he wrote about the police in his autobiography, the local dope squad or detectives were very familiar with him. Also, Malcolm X took pains to discuss in his autobiography why he considered himself a true hustler on the streets of Harlem, in which he wrote that he was surviving by his wits: "I was a true hustler—uneducated, unskilled at anything honorable."[27]

Although Malcolm X was no longer a member of Muhammad's NOI, all of the foregoing details were published in his autobiography to show how, in the end, the NOI saved his life. At the time that he and Haley started work on the autobiography, Malcolm still held the Honorable Elijah Muhammad in the highest regard. That, in fact, was why he sought Muhammad's permission to write the book. That too was the reason that after being suspended publicly by Muhammad over what the NOI leader considered to be insensitive comments about the 1963 Kennedy assassination, Malcolm still had positive things to say about Muhammad. As Haley wrote, Malcolm told him—shortly before he broke away from the NOI—that he respected Muhammad so much that anything that he did was fine with him, adding: "I'm always hurt over any act of disobedience on my part concerning Mr. Muhammad."[28]

According to Haley's epilogue, toward the end in mid-February 1965, barely a week before his death, Malcolm made it known to close associates that he had the suspicion that his own Muslim brothers in his former NOI organization were after him. Therefore, in a final interview with *Life* magazine correspondent Gordon Parks on February 18, 1965, he made several comments about threats against his life. When Parks asked Malcolm if it was really true that there were killers after him, he said it was, and that hired killers had already tried twice, in a week, to kill him. When Parks asked about seeking possible police protection, Malcolm laughed, and he went on to tell the *Life* correspondent that only a Muslim could protect a fellow Muslim because, as he put it, he knew the rules of the game when it came to Muslim tactics, adding: "I know. I invented many of those tactics."[29]

All of the foregoing details given by Haley in his epilogue in Malcolm's autobiography did make it seem that, indeed, Muhammad's NOI would be suspected in the assassination of Malcolm X on February 21, 1965. After the assassination, Haley wrote that on long-distance telephones, news reporters managed to reach the Chicago mansion that was

the headquarters of the Honorable Elijah Muhammad to seek answers
to their questions about Malcolm X, as they were anxious to interview
him. Yet Muhammad would not come to the phone. Instead, an NOI
spokesman announced that Muhammad had no immediate comment,
and that he would make one later. Meanwhile, by Haley's account, by
the evening of February 21, some hours after the assassination, many
black men and women gathered at Louis Michaux's bookstore, where
many of Harlem's blacks often congregated. Also, OAAU members reportedly opened their Hotel Theresa headquarters and went inside to
sit down without making any comments. While the local newspapers,
including the *New York Daily News*, came out the next day with ban-
ner headlines about Malcolm X's assassination, it was also reported in
the local newspapers that Malcolm X's oldest child, Atallah, had written a one-liner letter to her dead father, which was quoted in Haley's
epilogue as: "Dear Daddy, I love you so. O dear, O dear, I wish you
wasn't dead."[30]

Malcolm X's autobiography has been very useful in a variety of ways,
including making readers aware of some of the societal happenings when
he was growing up as well as crucial details about his life in general and,
in particular, his Islamic beliefs. What Haley underscored about the
assassination has been corroborated to indicate that Muhammad and
his NOI were suspected of involvement. For example, Professor Claude
Andrew Clegg III of Indiana University, in *An Original Man: The
Life and Times of Elijah Muhammad*, wrote that the NOI leader might
not have given an explicit order for the assassination of Malcolm X
that resulted in what he described as Malcolm X's gangland-style assassination. Yet, as he added, Muhammad seemed to have made it very
clear through editorials, telephone conversations, and his tolerance of
Muslim youth violence that "the slaying of the former minister had his
implicit support."[31]

Although Malcolm X died on that fateful February 21st day, when
he was gunned down, his posthumously published autobiography
helps readers to know that several aspects of Malcolm's travels and
lifelong activities do show both the spiritual and physical aspects of
the significant changes that he went through. The book also goes a
long way to help readers to come to terms with the fact that, in the
last two years of his life, Malcolm X's travels were part of the way

that he sought knowledge and international acknowledgment of his total existence. Given his national and international stature, many officials felt that, when Malcolm X was shot and killed, he was to be treated as a heroic figure by the medical examiners and officialdom. Instead, as Haley painfully wrote in his epilogue to *The Autobiography of Malcolm X*, the famous Muslim leader's body was still listed in the morgue as "John Doe"—as required by law—because he had not formally been identified by his next of kin, his spouse, Betty Shabazz. For an autopsy and formal identification, Haley reported that Malcolm X's body was moved to the office of Dr. Milton Helpern, New York's Chief City Medical Examiner, who confirmed in his report that shotgun pellet wounds in the heart had, in fact, killed Malcolm X, and that there was a total of 13 wounds, which showed that he was shot 13 times with either a .38 or .45 caliber gun. As required by law, Malcolm's wife, accompanied by attorney Percy Sutton, visited the offices of the medical examiner, where a positive identification of her husband was to be made by her. Others present included Mrs. Ella Collins, Malcolm's half-sister, and Mr. Joseph E. Halls, the general manager of the Unity Funeral Home in Harlem, which was to handle the funeral arrangements for the family.[32]

After Malcolm X's death, the American public began to see the resilience and strength of his widow. Although pregnant with twins at the time and in mourning, she showed that she was a formidable woman when she agreed to make a statement after coming from the funeral home. As reported by Haley in his epilogue, she lamented the fact that when her husband talked about his life being in peril, it was not taken seriously, and that when their home was firebombed, the insinuation was that he did it himself. At that point, she asked if Malcolm X also shot himself to seek fame, as it had been reported about the arson that took place in their home. Meanwhile, although Muslims believed in a speedy burial of their dead members, Haley reported in his epilogue that, this time around, Betty and her family announced on February 22 that for a properly planned funeral for her famous husband, the funeral services would be delayed for five days, and the Unity Funeral Home was duly informed. Subsequently, Betty visited the funeral home to select a casket made for a tall person: a six-foot, nine-inch casket. It was also announced to reporters that the body of Malcolm X would be dressed in a business suit, and that it would be put on view under a glass shield for four days, but the final funeral services would be at a local church.[33]

Malcolm X's February 27, 1965, funeral at the Faith Temple Church of Christ attracted local, national, and international mourners, with tributes coming from political, Islamic, and civic leaders. The task of giving the eulogy fell on his friend, Ossie Davis, the famous actor, who did not waste time to describe Malcolm as a shining prince, who did not hesitate to die for all of us because, as Davis put it, he loved us all. He gave several attributes of Malcolm, which made him stand out among men and women of his generation. He saw the funeral audience as the people of Harlem coming "to bid farewell to one of its brightest hopes—extinguished now, and gone from us forever."[34]

Apart from Malcolm's impact as an Islamic leader who preached in mosques, many commentators, including CBS correspondent Mike Wallace, pointed out that he did use his public speeches to shed light on unfair discriminatory practices. Therefore, it should also be fair to say that while Malcolm did not participate in the civil rights circles like Dr. King and his lieutenants did with marches and protests, he did equally impact the overall civil rights movement by helping to expose racism and unfair practices that led to significant changes through legislative measures. They included the passing of the 1964 Civil Rights Act, whose debate King and Malcolm X came to witness and, as a result, met face-to-face for the first time in the U.S. Capitol on March 26, 1964.

The impact of Malcolm X's life and death is also seen in the fact that streets, boulevards, and even alleys in several prominent cities bear his name. In New York, Harlem's Lenox Avenue was renamed Malcolm X Boulevard. In several states as far apart as New York, Texas, and Michigan, streets and educational institutions bear the name of Malcolm X, decades after his death. Several cities, including Washington, D.C., and Berkeley, California, have, since the 1970s, also honored Malcolm X's legacy by proclaiming his birthday as a citywide day of celebration. Furthermore, Malcolm's importance in the annals of American and world history became apparent in 1992, when Gregory Reed, an important manuscript collector, purchased the original manuscript of Malcolm X's autobiography for $100,000 at the sale of items from the estate of Alex Haley. Above all, Malcolm X's oldest daughter—Atallah Shabazz—

asserted it in the best possible way in her foreword to the 1999 edition of her father's autobiography, when she described her father's impact in the following words: "My father affected Americans—black and white—in untold measure and not always in ways as definitive as census charts and polls have dictated."[35]

It is true that Malcolm X has impacted Americans of all walks of life in a variety of ways. Also, locally and internationally, he continues to be a force to reckon with in social, cultural, and intellectual circles in unimaginable ways. That is why one would assume that with his death, which took place almost half a century ago in 1965, public interest in him would wane considerably by now. Yet, *The Autobiography of Malcolm X* has, in fact, been translated into Japanese, and several other countries in Asia, the Middle East, and Africa have been contemplating the translation of Malcolm's life story into such foreign languages as Chinese (Mandarin), Russian, Arabic, and also into African languages like Swahili and Hausa. In that way, the autobiography can reach many more readers. It has as well been shown in recorded and tracking accounts of international booksellers that Malcolm's autobiography sells more than 150,000 copies a year locally, nationally, and internationally. Above all, the Harlem-based Schomburg Center for Research in Black Culture—which is an important unit of the New York Public Library that currently houses some of the historic papers of Malcolm X—is visited each day that the center is open by numerous researchers, teachers, students, and curious tourists. According to employees of the center, most of the visitors come to the center to amass needed research materials to do school and publishable work about the assassinated black Muslim leader as well as human and civil rights activist by the famous name of Malcolm X.[36]

MALCOLM X: HIS OVERALL LEGACY IN HISTORY

Immediately following Malcolm X's death, some people suggested that dying at such a young age, Malcolm would have no appreciable legacy. Such naysayers were answered by Morehouse College President Emeritus Benjamin Elijah Mays, an ordained minister and scholar, who would give the eulogy at Dr. King's funeral four days after his April 4, 1968, assassination. Dr. Mays, who was president of Morehouse College when

King was an undergraduate student, was trying to respond to mourners and editorial commentators, who also felt that Dr. King had died too young. Mays agreed that it was tragic that King died very young, indeed at 39 years of age, like Malcolm. However, he went on to point out that several important world figures died young, yet they carved niches for themselves and also left lasting legacies. He gave as examples the deaths of the following notable people and the years they lived: Jesus Christ at 33 years; Joan of Arc at 19 years; Byron and Burns at 36 years; Keats and Marlowe at 29 years; mournful poet Shelley at 30 years; black poet, novelist, and playwright Paul Laurence Dunbar before 34 years; assassinated president John F. Kennedy at 46 years; and Yale-educated academician William Rainey Harper at 49 years. Dr. Mays then underscored to a loud applause and also to the delight of Dr. King's funeral audience that, as he had said often, it was what one accomplished for mankind that mattered most, and that "it isn't how long one lives, but how well."[37]

For example, having lived 39 years, Dr. King still left such a lasting legacy that today, the United States has honored his memory in a variety of ways, including having one of the nation's national holidays named in honor of his birthday. Unlike King, Malcolm X has yet to have any national holiday named in his honor, but he has left a lasting legacy that, from all indications, many Americans and people throughout the world have cherished. In February of each year, African Americans of all walks of life are joined by their foreign and nonblack friends, colleagues, and collaborators to celebrate Black History Month, during which leaders of black struggles, before and after the historic Emancipation Proclamation of President Abraham Lincoln, are celebrated. At this time, the popular names that invariably pop up are those of such black leaders as Frederick Douglass, Martin Luther King, Jr., and Rosa Parks, among several others. Although Malcolm X does not have either a holiday named after him or a recognizable local and international award aligned with his name, it is still agreed that he deserves to be remembered, and that several events created around his name—including the heritage postal stamp issued on January 20, 1999, in his honor—make sure that Malcolm X is counted among the notable black leaders of the 20th century. Therefore, to the delight of his admirers and family members,

Malcolm has very often been counted among black men and women whose names command respect and admiration. Most certainly, Malcolm X died young, but his name—as either Malcolm X or as El-Hajj Malik El-Shabazz—invariably comes up whenever Americans begin to celebrate an admixture of black and white leaders who lived purposeful lives and went onto become symbols of hope and admiration. From his speeches and writings, Malcolm later regretted that, while serving as a leader within the Honorable Elijah Muhammad's NOI, he acted in such sycophantic ways that he was often seen as a mere rabble rouser, who invoked as much hatred as other embittered black men and women of America. At the time, one particular speech, full of hatred and for which he was sadly known, was titled "The Ballot or the Bullet." He gave the speech on April 3, 1964, in which he told his audience that he was not in the presence of his audience to deliver his speech as an American or as either a patriot or a flag-saluting citizen. Instead, he emphasized that he was speaking as a victim of the American system as well as seeing the United States through the eyes of the victimized, adding provocatively that, in a contrast to the dream of which Dr. King, in his nonviolent approach to civil rights, so eloquently spoke, he—Malcolm X—did not see any American dream, but instead only an "American nightmare."[38]

Yet, by early 1965, Malcolm X had reexamined his rhetorical language and come to the realization that he knew better as the mature El-Hajj Malik El-Shabazz (or Malcolm Shabazz). Therefore, he wanted to go down in history as the new or reinvented Malcolm X, who now eschewed violence in its varied forms. In his new, reawakened life, Malcolm X broke with his past, which included the NOI and its message of separatism and hate, while still urging his fellow blacks to see pride in their race as well as their African ancestry. At this time, which was barely a year before his untimely death, Malcolm X in fact went on to complain about lack of brotherhood in American society, and that he no longer wanted the United States to be led by leaders who believed in separatism as well as inequality and injustice—clamoring for justice for all Americans.[39]

Followers and supporters of Malcolm X were happy that he was such a changed man that he would no longer deride Dr. Martin Luther King, Jr., and other civil rights leaders, whose 1963 March on

Washington he had previously, as an NOI leader, ridiculed as "the farce on Washington." Malcolm X had changed so dramatically that his first meeting with Dr. King in March 1964 was in a spirit of cordiality and mutual respect. Very significantly, James Baldwin, the well-known black writer, commented on the King–Malcolm relationship in positive terms. That was why, in quoting Baldwin as part of his assessment of both King and Malcolm X, James H. Cone wrote that because of the profound mutual respect and the tremendous impact that each had upon the other's thinking, "by the time each met his death, there was practically no difference between them."[40]

Malcolm's visits to the African continent made him so conversant with African liberation history that he started to quote aspects of it in his speeches—a situation that would leave Malcolm an enviable legacy in black history and pan-Africanism. James H. Cone, for example, recalled how Malcolm X listened to complaints of Mississippi-born Fannie Lou Hammer, one of the leaders of the Mississippi Freedom Democratic Party (MFDP), that she and other black leaders were beaten brutally in their native Mississippi merely for making the efforts to register fellow blacks to be able to vote. At a Harlem rally of several hundred OAAU members, Malcolm X was so irritated by what happened in Mississippi to Hammer and her fellow black leaders that he invoked the name of an African nationalist organization, by telling the Harlem rally in these words: "We need a 'Mau Mau' to win freedom and equality for Negroes [blacks] in the United States."[41]

Having visited Kenya, where the Mau Mau operated, Malcolm X knew about them as a revolutionary group of Africans in the Kenyan nationalist liberation struggle, who led an armed revolt against the British colonial rule in the East African nation, whose very radical anti-British methods so much impressed Malcolm X that he later described the Mau Mau as "the greatest freedom fighters in Africa."[42]

Several black scholars and professionals have seen wisdom in Malcolm X's legacy of toughness, especially where he called for reciprocal toughness in dealing with situations in which blacks, in nonviolent protests, had been attacked, maimed, brutalized, or even killed by armed white police officers and their trained bulldogs. Dr. Kenneth Clark, a black scholar active in the American civil rights movement, did not deem it necessary to come out to endorse Malcolm X's call for toughness in dealing with their opponents. Yet, Dr. Clark pointed out that he saw a measure of danger in the advocacy of black men and women showing love toward their enemies. As a trained psychologist, he further observed that the call for blacks to love their enemies or opponents in their quest for human and civil rights could create what he described as the "psychological burden too great for oppressed blacks."[43]

Malcolm X had very similar interests and goals to those of Martin Luther King, Jr., but both black leaders differed in their approaches and their respective styles of implementation. Yet, Professor Clark did point out publicly that he agreed with Malcolm X's analysis of why, for many years, white liberals supported Dr. King's idea of nonviolence. Furthermore, Professor Clark disclosed how very disturbing it was for any meaningful black leader to reflect on the possibility that the love-thy-neighbor and nonviolence aspects of Dr. King's philosophy was receiving such a widespread and uncritical acceptance among several moderate and liberal whites mostly because, as the past history of enslaved blacks showed, that was "not inconsistent with the stereotype of the Negro as a meek, long-suffering creature, who prays for deliverance but who rarely acts decisively against injustice."[44]

Malcolm X's legacy includes the fact that toward the end of his life, he had toned down his rhetoric and his stringent criticism of white people. After all, he was no longer in the NOI, where such thinking was commonplace. Yet, several scholars—including Dr. Cone—have concluded that part of Malcolm's legacy has come to include the fact that, in place of the history of integration as well as nonviolence and love of one's enemy, "Malcolm would be remembered as having initially advocated separation self-defense, and self-love."[45]

However, many Americans still remembered that in a 1963 *New York Times* interview with Dr. Kenneth Clark, about two years before his assassination, Malcolm X, then still a Muslim radical, had criticized Dr. King for what he saw as disarming blacks in their struggle for human and civil rights. In the words of Malcolm, King could be seen as the best agent or even weapon that white people have, especially when it came to a situation in which such whites were ready to brutalize black men and women. As Malcolm pointed out in the interview, Dr. King's nonviolent philosophy was paramount in civil rights protests, which Malcolm saw as effectively telling blacks not to defend themselves. Yet, he felt that "self-defense was both a rational act and a moral responsibility."[46]

Professor Clegg, in *An Original Man: The Life and Times of Elijah Muhammad*, unequivocally saw how Malcolm X's legacy would be advanced or protected because of the remarkable way that his pilgrimage to Mecca helped him to turn a new leaf. Apart from giving Malcolm an opportunity to turn things around to buttress his image, the pilgrimage, in Dr. Clegg's estimation, also gave Malcolm an "out"—that it saved the ex-NOI member from appearing to be opportunistic as well as merely pretending to be a true Muslim. Instead, as the author further pointed out, Malcolm X's positive actions, as a Muslim, made Muslims and non-Muslims see the faults of Elijah Muhammad as the NOI's supreme leader. For example, Professor Clegg pointed out that with Malcolm going out of his way in "portraying the [*hajj*] journey as a spiritual awakening, he laid the burden of his Nation of Islam past at the feet of Elijah Muhammad."[47]

Malcolm X strategically had the sum total of his future accomplishments in mind. That was why he wanted his legacy to portray the fact that, before his pilgrimage, he had been fooled by the NOI leader for not less than two decades. He attributed that to being gullible as well as acting in good faith. Thankfully, his trip to Mecca helped him to see, as Professor Clegg pointed out, the color-blindness of the Muslim world's human society. Thereafter, he could discard the racial Islam that he had been taught to promulgate in the past. However, he was glad that in the process, he "always kept an open mind in my intelligent search for truth."[48]

The followers and admirers of Malcolm were happy that things were falling so much into place for him that even those who had traditionally ignored him up till now no longer saw him as the racist bent on the destruction of his opponents, including whites that he had before now considered to be devils. Therefore, the public began to welcome the change they saw in Malcolm X as a positive thing. For a progressive legacy, Clegg wrote that, at the time, Malcolm X could have the best of both worlds, adding that he now had a totally new image that was

untainted by the black supremacy label that the press and others had
stuck on the black Muslim movement as well as "a ready-made con-
stituency of black nationalists and disgruntled civil rights activists."[49]

An important legacy Malcolm left toward the end of his life was that
when Muhammad and other NOI leaders were trying to portray him
in bad light, he kept his peace by remaining calm. Although Malcolm
did that to show his supporters and admirers that he was a changed
person, and that he was not living in the past, Muhammad and his NOI
leadership however knew that any open conflict with Malcolm X could
be very hard as well as very much embarrassing for their camp. At this
point, Malcolm showed the legacy of being a mature Islamic leader for
the OAAU and the MMI that he led. Malcolm comported himself so
much that he received praise from several people, although his critics
within the NOI felt that he was receiving accolades or recognition that
he did not deserve.[50]

An important legacy that Malcolm bequeathed to his followers
within the OAAU and the MMI organizations was that anyone who
wanted to lead others like the Honorable Elijah Muhammad was doing
must first learn how to live a clean and honorable life. The reason for
such an admonition or exemplary way of living was that two former
secretaries to Muhammad by the name of Evelyn Williams and Lucille
Rosary claimed publicly and also filed paternity suits in a Los Angeles
court against Muhammad that he had children out of wedlock with
them.[51]

In less than a year from these events, Malcolm X would be assassinated, but his character remained so unblemished that it added to
the valuable legacy that his widow and children would be proud of. For
example, among details that would taint Muhammad's legacy was part
of the revelation in the Los Angeles Court, as published in the Harlem-
based *Amsterdam News* July 11, 1964, that Ms. Williams charged the
Honorable Elijah Muhammad with fathering her four-year old daughter by the name of Eva Marie, and that Ms. Rosary too claimed in
court papers that Muhammad had fathered all of her three daughters,
namely four-year old Saudi, two-year old Lisha, and a baby girl born in
early July 1964. Compared to Muhammad, Malcolm had a solid and
admirable reputation that would remain intact even after his assassination. Therefore, many Americans were not surprised that he received

national and international honors after his death, including a postal stamp being issued by the U.S. Postal Service in his honor. To try to come close to the enviable legacy that Malcolm X was to leave behind after his death, NOI leaders desperately instructed two spokespersons by the names of Raymond Sharieff and John Ali to issue public denials that "their leader [Muhammad] would not dignify the charges by answering them."[52]

A very useful legacy in organizational leadership that Malcolm X showed in the black community of America was that once a leader demonstrates integrity, he becomes so popular to the general public that he receives a massive following. That was why Malcolm X was so well respected that upon Muhammad's disgrace in court, a large number of NOI members resigned their membership in order to flock to Malcolm's OAAU and MMI organizations—actions which made Muhammad and his followers both nervous and angry. People close to the NOI inner circles knew how angry Muhammad was at the time. In fact, Professor Clegg further disclosed from his research for his book on Muhammad that an adviser working for Malcolm X, with access to the Nation's inner circle, disclosed that "orders to have him [Malcolm] murdered were issued from Chicago around the time that reporters were printing the Williams-Rosary stories."[53]

Professor Clegg, being privy to information from Muhammad's NOI circles, further wrote that Muhammad and his NOI leadership did not want to see Malcolm X alive, as the American public began to compare the two leaders of the NOI and the OAAU. It was, therefore, not surprising that Malcolm X left such a respectable legacy after his assassination that, in Omaha, Nebraska, for example, the Malcolm X family home on 3448 Pinkney Street marks the site where Malcolm and his family first lived, and the site has, since 1984, been listed on the National Registry of Historic Places.[54]

As part of the overall soaring legacy of Malcolm X, a Michigan Historical marker was put up in 1975 to mark his childhood home site in the state. To do more to honor the name of Malcolm X, the elementary school that he attended in Michigan as a youngster is also now known as the El-Hajj Malik El-Shabazz Academy (sometimes referred to simply as Malcolm X Academy), which is a public charter school that focuses on Afrocentric thematic curriculum. While the honors keep on coming Malcolm X's way, several Americans have very often wondered why nothing had been done to honor the name or activities of the Honorable Elijah Muhammad, the very man who helped Malcolm X to reinvent himself after his imprisonment by being warmly welcomed by the NOI leader as a new convert of the black Muslim group. On some occasions, some of Muhammad's followers have wickedly pointed to Malcolm's imprisonment as a reason why he should not be so publicly honored. It was to counter the NOI leadership revelations about Malcolm that the supporters of the OAAU leader revealed that Muhammad had also been convicted of draft evasion on December 18, 1942, by a District of Columbia tribunal, and that he was sentenced to serve a jail term of not less than one calendar year at the Federal Correctional Institution (FCI) at Milan, Michigan—an imprisonment that Muhammad started serving with effect from July 23, 1943.[55]

Malcolm X in 1965, shortly before his assassination. (Library of Congress)

That was how, in the end, Muhammad and his NOI associates have been silenced to the point that they could no longer use the imprisonment of Malcolm, which happened when he was relatively very young, to impugn or blackmail the OAAU leader. Compared to Muhammad's tattered image, Malcolm's well-cultivated clean adult life has always pointed to his enduring and admired legacy, which has gone a long way to confirm for Americans of today and of Malcolm's generation that— to paraphrase the words of Morehouse president Emeritus Mays—it is not simply how long one lives that matters in helping to create a viable or lasting legacy in today's world but, indeed, how well. Therefore, no matter what Muhammad and his NOI leadership tried to plot as part of desperate final efforts to tarnish the image of Malcolm X after his 1968 assassination, the black community in particular and Americans in general did not pay much attention to such belated plots. That was why Malcolm X's legacy remained so intact that various positive public actions have been taken to honor his memory and, indeed, his name. Honors for Malcolm have included various major researchers and college students continuing to write books as well as campus theses and dissertations about the late OAAU and MMI leader. The publication of Marable's 2011 vast biography of 594 pages of the assassinated OAAU leader is one of the latest examples. In contrast, the Honorable Elijah Muhammad—as Malcolm's major opponent since he left the NOI—became so unpopular that, according to biographer Clegg, when Muhammad was seriously ill in the spring of 1975, he had to use an alias—instead of his real name—to enter Chicago's Mercy Hospital, where on the morning of February 25, the NOI leader, according to Clegg, was diagnosed to be suffering from several serious illnesses, including congestive heart failure, and he "was pronounced dead at the age of seventy-seven."[56]

NOTES

FRONT MATTER

1. From Ossie Davis's eulogy preached at Malcolm X's funeral on February 27, 1965.

2. Attallah Shabazz, "Foreword," in Malcolm X, with Alex Haley, *The Autobiography of Malcolm X* (New York: Ballantine Books, 1999), xi.

3. Ibid.

4. From Ossie Davis's eulogy of February 27, 1965.

CHAPTER 1

1. Malcolm X with Alex Haley, *The Autobiography of Malcolm X* (New York: Ballantine Books, 1999), 1.

2. Ibid., 153.

3. James H. Madison, *A Lynching in the Heartland: Race and Memory in America* (New York: Palgrave-Macmillan of St. Martin's Press, 2001), introduction, 1.

4. Nell Irvin Painter, *Creating Black Americans: African American History, 1619 to Present* (New York: Oxford University Press, 2006), 295.

5. Editor, *The New York Times*, July 15, 2010, B16.

6. Ibid.

7. Malcolm X with Alex Haley, *The Autobiography of Malcolm X*, 14.

8. Ibid., 25.

9. Ibid., 45.

10. Ibid., 48.

CHAPTER 2

1. Manning Marable, *A Life of Reinvention: Malcolm X* (New York: Viking, 2011), 64.

2. Ibid.

3. Ibid., 64–65.

4. Ibid., 65–66.

5. Ibid., 64–65.

6. Ibid., 68.

7. Claude Andrew Clegg, III, *An Original Man: The Life and Times of Elijah Muhammad* (New York: St. Martin's Press, 1997), 105.

8. Malcolm X with Alex Haley, *Autobiography of Malcolm X, As Told To Alex Haley*, introduction.

9. Clegg III, *An Original Man*.

10. Ibid., 109; Malcolm X, *Autobiography*, 196–97; Clegg III, *An Original Man*, 197.

11. Clegg III, *An Original Man*, 106–7.

12. Ibid., 107–8.

13. Ibid., 108.

14. Marable, *A Life of Reinvention*, 107.

15. Walter Dean Myers, *Malcolm X: Any Means Necessary* (New York: Scholastic Press, 1993), 97.

16. Ibid.

17. Malcolm X with Alex Haley, *Autobiography of Malcolm X*; Walter Dean Myles, *Malcolm X*, 99.

18. Marable, *A Life of Reinvention*, 138.

19. Ibid., 140–41.

20. Ibid., 145.

21. Ibid., 145–46.

22. Ibid.

23. Ibid., 115–16.

24. Ibid., 250.

25. Ibid., 399.

26. Ibid., 7.

27. Ibid., 7–8.

28. Clegg III, *An Original Man*, 192.

29. Ibid., *194*.

30. Marable, *A Life of Reinvention*, 182.

31. Ibid.

32. Ibid.

33. Ibid., 183–84.

34. Clegg III, *An Original Man*, 199.

35. Ibid., 195–96.

36. Ibid., 197.

37. Ibid., 198.

38. Malcolm X with Alex Haley, *The Autobiography of Malcolm X*, 296.

39. Ibid., 297.

40. Ibid., 297–98.

41. Ibid., 299.

42. Ibid.

43. Ibid., 300.

44. Ibid.

45. Ibid., 300–301.

46. Clegg III, *An Original Man*, 198–99.

47. Ibid., 199–200.

48. Ibid., 201–2.

49. Ibid., 203–4.

CHAPTER 3

1. Clegg, III, *An Original Man*, 210–11.

2. Bruce Perry,. *Malcolm X: The Life a Man Who Changed Black America* (Barrytown, NY: Station Hill, 1991), 212.

3. Clegg, *An Original Man*, 184–85.

4. Ibid., 219.

5. Ibid., 188.

6. Ibid.

7. Ibid., 186–87.

8. Ibid., 212.

9. Marable, *A Life of Reinvention*, 298.

10. Clegg, *An Original Man*, 213.

11. Perry, *Malcolm X*, 231.

12. Clegg, *An Original Man*, 233.

13. Ibid., 212–13.

14. Marable, *A Life of Reinvention*, 360–61.

15. Ibid., 307–8.

16. Ibid., 308–9.

17. Ibid., 308.

18. Perry, *Malcolm X*, 268–69.

19. Marable, *A Life of Reinvention*, 316–17.

20. Ibid., 316–17.

21. The title of Professor Manning Marable's 2011 book contains a subtitle "A Life of Reinvention."

22. Marable, *A Life of Reinvention*, 365–66.

23. Ibid., 366.

24. Ibid., 366.

25. Clegg, *An Original Man*, 216–17.

26. Ibid., 149–50; also in Marable, *A Life of Reinvention*, 80, 399–400.

27. Clegg, *An Original Man*, 70–71.

28. Marable, *A Life of Reinvention*, 316–17.

29. Ibid., 341.

30. Ibid., 91.

31. Kwame Nkrumah, *Ghana: Autobiography of Kwame Nkrumah* (London: Thomas Nelson and Sons, 1957).

32. Marable, *A Life of Reinvention*, 240–41.

33. James H. Cone, *Martin & Malcolm & America: A Dream or a Nightmare* (Maryknoll, New York: Orbis Books, 1991), 270.

34. Marable, *A Life of Reinvention*, 136.

35. Ibid., 340–41.

36. Ibid., 341.

CHAPTER 4

1. Marable, *Malcolm X*, 158.

2. Ibid., 159.

3. A.B. Assensoh, *African Political Leadership* (Melbourne, Florida: Krieger Publishing Company, 1996), 20–21; A. B. Assensoh, *Rev. Dr. Martin Luther King, Jr., and America's Quest for Racial Integration* (Ifracombe, Devon, UK: Arthur H. Stockwell Ltd., 1987), 27.

4. Kevin Gaines, *American Africans in Ghana* (Chapel Hill, NC: University of North Carolina Press, 2006), 36.

5. Marable, *A Life of Reinvention*, 361.

6. Ibid., 314.

7. Ibid., 361.

8. Ibid., 370–71.

9. Ibid., 384.

10. Ibid.

11. Ibid., 384–85.

12. Clegg, III, *An Original Man*, 110.

13. Michael Friedly, *Malcolm X: The Assassination* (New York: Carroll & Graf Publishers, 1992), 67.

14. Ibid.

15. Ibid., 67–68.

16. Ibid., 68.

17. Ibid.

18. Ibid.

19. Ibid., 69.

20. Marable, *A Life of Reinvention*, 361–62.

21. Ibid., 375.

22. Chinua Achebe, *There Was a Country: A Personal History of Biafra* (New York: The Penguin Press, 2012), 95–96; also Marable, *A Life of Reinvention*, 374.

23. Marable, *A Life of Reinvention*, 374.

24. Ibid.

25. Ibid.

26. Ibid., 375.

27. Ibid., 376.

28. Ibid., 378.

29. Ibid., 379–80.

30. Ibid., 381.

31. Ibid.

32. Friedly, *Malcolm X*, 72–73.

33. Ibid.

34. Clegg, III, *The Price of Liberty* (Chapel Hill, NC: University of North Carolina Press, 1998), 15–16.

35. Marable, *A Life of Reinvention*, 385–86.

CHAPTER 5

1. Malcolm X with Alex Haley, *The Autobiography of Malcolm X*, 464.
2. Ibid.
3. Ibid., 465.
4. Clegg, III, *An Original Man*, 216–17.
5. Clayborne Carson, *Malcolm X: The FBI File* (New York: Carroll & Graf Publishers, Inc., 1991), 39–40.
6. Marable, *A Life of Reinvention*, 12–13.
7. Ibid., 219–20.
8. Ibid., 329.
9. Ibid., 372.
10. Ibid., 68.
11. Friedly, *Malcolm X*, 67–68.
12. Malcolm X, *The Autobiography of Malcolm X*, 416.
13. Marable, *A Life of Reinvention*, 416.
14. Ibid., 418.
15. Ibid., 418–19.
16. Ibid., 419–20.
17. Ibid., 420.
18. Ibid., 421.
19. Ibid., 422.
20. Ibid., 423.
21. Ibid., 427–28.
22. Ibid., 433.
23. Friedly, *Malcolm X*, 30–31.
24. Ibid., 36–37.
25. Ibid., 38.
26. Ibid., 52–53.
27. Ibid.
28. Ibid., 53.

EPILOGUE

1. Malcolm X with Alex Haley, *The Autobiography of Malcolm X*, 346–48.

2. A. B. Assensoh, *Rev. Dr. Martin Luther King, Jr. and America's Quest for Racial Integration* (Ilfracombe, Devon, UK: Arthur H. Stockwell Ltd., 1987), introduction; Lawrence D. Reddick, *Crusader without Violence: A Biography of Martin Luther King, Jr.* (New York: Harper & Row, 1959), 160–61; Clayborne Carson., ed., *The Autobiography of Martin Luther King, Jr.* (New York: Warner Books, 1998), editor's introduction.

3. A. B. Assensoh, *Kwame Nkrumah: Six Years in Exile, 1966–1972* (Ilfracombe, Devon, UK: Arthur H. Stockwell Ltd., 1978), 27–28; Kwame Nkrumah, *Ghana: Autobiography of Kwame Nkrumah* (London: Thomas Nelson and Sons, 1978), 4–5; Nnamdi Azikiwe, *My Odyssey: Autobiography* (London: C. Hurst, 1970), author's preface.

4. Clegg, III, *An Original Man*, 107–8.

5. Douglas Martin, "Death of Percy Sutton," *The New York Times*, December 26, 2009, A1.

6. Marable, *A Life of Reinvention*, 458–59.

7. Kwame Nkrumah, *Ghana* 180–82. Also in St. Clair Drake, "The American Negro's Relation to Africa," *Africa Today*, 14, No. 6 (December 1967), 12–15.

8. Malcolm X with Alex Haley, *The Autobiography of Malcolm X*, 378–79.

9. Clegg III, *An Original Man*, 135–40.

10. Malcolm X with Alex Haley, *The Autobiography of Malcolm X*, foreword, xiii–iv.

11. Ibid., 464–66.

12. Ibid.

13. Marable, *A Life of Reinvention*, 421.

14. Ibid., 421–22.

15. Ibid., 423.

16. Ibid., 472.

17. K. Gregory, "Words of Praise for Malcolm X's Grandson," *The New York Times*, May 13, 2013, A1.

18. "Justice Clarence Thomas has made his imprint on Supreme Court," Juan Williams article, http://www.foxnews.com/opinion/2011/10/22/after-20-justice-clarence-thomas-has-made-his-imprint-on-supreme-court/#ixzz2VmgzeTiJ.

19. Malcolm X with Alex Haley, *The Autobiography of Malcolm X*, foreword, ix.

20. Ibid.

21. Ibid., epilogue.

22. Ibid.

23. James H. Cone, *Martin & Malcolm & America: A Dream or a Nightmare* (New York: Orbis Books, 1991), 315–16.

24. Marable, *A Life of Reinvention*, 219–20.

25. Ibid., 9–11.

26. Malcolm X with Alex Haley, *The Autobiography of Malcolm X*, 397–98.

27. Ibid., 111.

28. Ibid., 413.

29. Ibid., 436.

30. Ibid., 446–47.

31. Clegg, *An Original Man*, 228.

32. Malcolm X with Alex Haley, *The Autobiography of Malcolm X*, 447.

33. Ibid., 447–48.

34. Ossie Davis, "Eulogy for Malcolm X," February 27, 1965.

35. Malcolm X with Alex Haley, *The Autobiography of Malcolm X*, foreword, xiii.

36. The visitors' log kept at the Schomburg Center for Research in Black Culture shows that many of the visitors visit to utilize the Malcolm X papers that his family has allowed to be deposited there. Also, Amazon.com and Barnes & Noble, as booksellers, have documented that over 150,000 copies of *The Autobiography of Malcolm X* are sold annually, and that the life story of Malcolm X has already been published in Japanese.

37. Coretta Scott King, *My Life with Martin Luther, King, Jr.* (New York: Holt, Rinehart and Winston, 1969), 357.

38. Malcolm X, "The Ballot or the Bullet" speech, given on April 3, 1964.

39. Editor, *The Socialist Newspaper, February 1965*, 6.

40. Cone, *Martin & Malcolm & America*, 259.

41. Ibid., 261.

42. Ibid., 262.

43. Ibid.

44. Ibid., 262–63; also in Kenneth Clark, "The New Negro in the North" in M. H. Ahmann, ed., *The New Negro* (Notre Dame, Indiana: Fides Publishers, 1961), 36–37.

45. Cone, *Martin & Malcolm & America*, 263.

46. Editorial Reporter, *The New York Times*, June 5, 1963, 23. Also in Cone, *Martin & Malcolm & America*, 264.

47. Clegg, *An Original Man*, 217.

48. Ibid.

49. Ibid.

50. Ibid., 219.

51. Ibid., 220–21.

52. Ibid., 220.

53. Ibid., 222.

54. National Register of Historic Places, Nebraska, Douglas County.

55. Clegg, *An Original Man*, 92–93.

56. Ibid., 275.

SELECTED BIBLIOGRAPHY

BOOKS

Abernathy, Ralph David. 1989. *And the Walls Came Tumbling Down: An Autobiography*. New York: Harper & Row.

Alexander, E. Curtis. 1989. *Elijah Muhammad on African-American Education*. New York: ECA Associates.

Assensoh, A. B. 1998. *African Political Leadership: Jomo Kenyatta, Kwame Nkrumah and Julius K. Nyerere*. Malabar, FL: Krieger Publishers.

Assensoh, A. B. 1978. *Kwame Nkrumah: Six Years in Exile, 1966–1972*. Ilfracombe, Devon, UK: Arthur H. Stockwell Ltd.

Assensoh, A. B. 1987. *Rev. Dr. Martin Luther King, Jr. and America's Quest for Racial Integration*. Ilfracombe, Devon, UK: Arthur H. Stockwell Limited.

Assensoh, A. B., & Yvette M. Alex-Assensoh. 2001. *African Military History and Politics*. New York: Palgrave Division of St. Martin's Press.

Azikiwe, Nnamdi. 1970. *My Odyssey: An Autobiography*. Westport, CT: Praeger.

Branch, Taylor. 1998. *Pillar of Fire: America in the King Years, 1963–1965*. New York: Simon and Schuster.

Breitman, George, editor. 1970. *By Any Means Necessary: Speeches, Interviews, and a Letter by Malcolm X*. New York: Pathfinder Press.

Breitman, George. 1967. *The Last Year of Malcolm X: The Evolution of a Revolutionary*. New York: Pathfinder Press.

Breitman, George, editor. 1990. *Malcolm X Speaks: Selected Speeches and Statements*. New York: Grove, Weidenfeld Publisher.

Breitman, George, Herman Porter, and Baxter Smith. 1976. *The Assassination of Malcolm X*. New York: Pathfinder Press.

Carson, Clayborne, editor. 1998. *The Autobiography of Martin Luther King, Jr*. New York: Warren Books, 1998.

Carson, Clayborne, editor. 1991. *Malcolm X: The FBI File*. New York: Carroll & Graf Publishers.

Cashman, Sean D. 1991. *African-Americans and the Quest for Civil rights, 1900–1990*. New York: New York University Press.

Clark, Steve, editor. 1992. *February 1965: The Final Speeches*. New York: Pathfinder Press.

Clark, Steve, editor. 1991. *Malcolm X Talks to Young People: Speeches in the United States, Britain, and Africa*. New Y: Pathfinder Press.

Clarke, John Henrik. 1990. *Malcolm X: The Man and His Times*. Trenton, NJ: Africa World Press.

Clegg, III, Claude Andrew. 1997. *An Original Man: The Life and Times of Elijah Muhammad* by Claude Clegg. New York: St. Martin's Press.

Dyson, Michael E. 1995. *Making Malcolm: The Myth & Meaning of Malcolm X*. New York: Oxford University Press.

El-Amin, Mustafa. 1991. *The Religion of Islam and the Nation of Islam: What Is the Difference?* Newark, NJ: El-Amin productions.

Epps, Archie, editor. 1991. *The Speeches of Malcolm X at Harvard*. New York: Morrow.

Esedebe, P. Olisanwuche. 1982. *Pan-Africanism: The Idea and Movement, 1776–1963*. Washington, DC: Howard University Press.

Essien-Udom, E.U. 1995. *Black Nationalism: A Search for an Identity in America*. Chicago: University of Chicago Press.

Friedly, Michael. 1992. *Malcolm X: The Assassination*. New York: Carroll & Graf.

Gaines, Kevin K. 2006. *American Africans in Ghana*. Chapel Hill, NC: University of North Carolina Press.

Gallen, David, editor. 1992. *Malcolm X as They Knew Him*. New York: Carroll and Graf.

Garrow, David J. 1986. *Bearing the Cross: Martin Luther King, Jr., and the Southern Christian Leadership Conference*. New York: Vintage Books.

Garvey, Marcus. 1987. *Marcus Garvey: Life & Lessons*. Edited by Robert A. Hill & Barbara Bair. Berkeley: University of California Press.

Garvey, Marcus. 1986. *Philosophy and Opinions of Marcus Garvey*. Edited by Amy Jacques-Garvey (1923 Reprint). New York: Atheneum.

Goldman, Peter. 1971. *The Life and Death of Malcolm X*. Urbana: University of Illinois Press.

Haley, Alex. 1974. *Roots*. New York: Vanguard Press.

Hedgeman, Anna A. 1964. *The Trumpet Sounds: A Memoir of Negro Leadership*. New York: Holt, Rinehart and Winston.

Jenkins, Robert L., and Mfanya D. Tryman, co-editors. 2002. *The Malcolm X Encyclopedia*. Westport, CT: Greenwood Press.

Karim, Imam Benjamin, editor. 1971. *The End of White World Supremacy: Four Speeches by Malcolm X*. New York: Monthly Review Press.

Kelley, Robin D. G. 2003. *Freedom Dreams: The Black Radical Imagination*. Boston, MA: Beacon Press.

Kelley, Robin D. G. 1994. *Race Rebels*. New York: Free Press.

Lomax, Louis E. 1962. *The Negro Revolt*. New York: Harper & Row.

Lomax, Louis E. 1987. *To Kill a Black Man*. Reprint. Los Angeles, CA: Halloway House.

Malcolm X (with Alex Haley). 1999. *The Autobiography of Malcolm X*. New York: Ballantine Books.

Malcolm X (with Alex Haley). 1991. *Malcolm X Talks to Young People*. New York: Pathfinder Press.

Malcolm X (with Alex Haley). 1967. *Malcolm X on Afro-American History*. New York: Merit Publishers.

Malcolm X (with Alex Haley). 1965. *Two Speeches by Malcolm X*. New York: Pathfinder Press.

Marable, Mannin. 2011. *Malcolm X: A Life of Reinvention*. New York: Viking Penguin Group (USA) Ltd.

Nkrumah, Kwame. 1957. *Ghana: The Autobiography of Kwame Nkrumah*. London: Thomas Nelson and Sons.

Painter, Nell Irvin. 2005. *Creating Black Americans: African American History, 1619 to the Present*. New York: Oxford University Press.

Perry, Bruce, editor. 1989. *The Last Speeches of Malcolm X*. New York: Pathfinder Press.

Perry, Bruce. *Malcolm: The Life of a Man Who Changed Black America*. Barrytown, NY: Station Hill Press.

Reddick, Lawrence D. 1959. *Crusader without Violence: Biography of Martin Luther King, Jr*. New York: Harper & Row.

Robeson, Paul. 1993. *Paul Robeson, Jr. Speaks to America*. New Brunswick, NJ: Rutgers University Press.

Sayles, William. 1994. *From Civil Rights to Black Liberation: Malcolm X and the Organization of Organization of Afro-American Unity*. Boston: South End Publishers.

Scott, Coretta. 1969. *My Life with Martin Luther King, Jr*. New York: Holt, Rinehart and Winston.

Tryman, Mfanya D. 2002. *The Malcolm X Encyclopedia*. Westport, CT: Greenwood Press.

PERIODICALS/PAMPHLETS

Allen, Jr., Ernest. "Satokata Takahashi and the Flowering of Black Nationalism." *Black Scholar Journal* 24.1 (Winter 1994: 23–46).

Ansari, Z. I. "Aspects of Black Muslim Theology." *Studia Islamica Journal* 53 (1981: 137–76).

Ansari, Z. I. "W.D. Muhammad: The Making of a Black Muslim Leader, 1933–1961." *American Journal of Islamic Social Sciences* 22 (December 1985: 245–62).

Barboza, Steven. "Muslims: A Divided Legacy." *Emerge Magazine* (April 1992: 26–32).

Battle, V. DuWayne. "The Influence of Al-Islam in America on the Black Community." *Black Scholar* 19 (January/February 1988: 33–41).

Brown, Warren & J.M. Stephens, Jr. "Police Probe Killings in Baton Rouge." *Jet Magazine* (January 1972: 6–9).

Editor. "Commentary: Elijah Muhammad's 13 Illegitimate Children Must Share Estate: Court." *Jet Magazine* (January 25, 1979: 8–9).

Haley, Alex. "Mr. Muhammad Speaks." *Readers Digest* (March 1969: 100–104).

Hatchett, John F. "The Moslem [Muslim] Influences among American Negroes." *Journal of Human relations* 10.4 (1962: 375–82).

Jones, Jr., Oliver. "The Black Muslim Movement and the American Constitutional System." *Journal of Black Studies* 13.4 (June 1983: 417–37).

Khalifa, H.K. 1988. *The Legacy of the Honorable Elijah Muhammad* (pamphlet). Newport News, VA: United Brothers Communications Systems.

Lightfoot, Claude. "Negro Nationalism and the Black Muslims." *Political Affairs Journal* 41.7 (July 1962: 3–20).

Lincoln, C. Eric. "The Meaning of Malcolm X." *Christian Century Magazine* (April 7, 1965: 431–33).

Massaquoi, Hans. "Mystery of Malcolm X." *Ebony Magazine* (December 1964: 38–48).

Parks, Gordon. "The Violent End of the Man Called Malcolm X." *Life Magazine* (March, 5, 1965: 26–31).

Russel, Carlos E. "Exclusive Interview with Malcolm X." *Liberator Magazine* (May 1964: 12–13).

Shabazz, Betty. "The Legacy of My Husband, Malcolm X." *Ebony Magazine* (June 1969: 172–74).

Smith, Christopher E. "Black Muslims and the Development of Prisoners' Rights." *Journal of Black Studies* 24.2 (December 1993: 131–46).

Tyler, L.L. "The Protestant Ethic among the Black Muslims." *Phylon* 27.1 (Spring 1966: 5–14).

White, Abbie. "Christian Elements in Negro American Muslim Religious Beliefs." *Phylon* 25.4 (Winter 1964: 382–88).

Wiley, Charles W. "Who Was Malcolm X?" *National Review* (March 23, 1965: 239–240).

Woodford, John. "Testing America's Promise of free Speech: Muhammad Speaks in the 1960s." *Voices of the African Diaspora Magazine* 7.3 (Fall 1991: 3–16).

AUDIO SOURCES: MALCOLM X

1959 On "Minister Malcolm X & Minister Wallace D. Muhammad" (85 minutes)

1960 "A Weekly Radio Broadcast: *Mr. Muhammad Speaks*" (51 minutes). Malcolm X speaks on the work and mission of the Hon. Elijah Muhammad.

May 1, 1962 "The Crisis of Racism": Malcolm X, James Farmer, William Worthy (15 minutes) .

December 1962 Malcolm X on *"The Black Man's History"* (87 minutes)

January 23, 1963 Malcolm X speaks on "The Race Problem in America" at the invitation of the African Students Association and the campus chapter of the NAACP, Michigan State University, East Lansing, MI (54 minutes)

June 1963 Malcolm X speaks on "The Black Revolution" at the invitation of Adam Clayton Powell, Abyssinian Baptist Church, New York City (26 minutes)

August 10, 1963 "Harlem Unity Rally" (116 minutes)

November 10, 1963 Malcolm X delivers a speech, titled "Message to the Grass Roots" (46 minutes). Northern Grass Roots Leadership Conference Detroit, Michigan

December 13, 1964 "OAAU Rally, Audubon Ballroom, New York City" (70 minutes). Malcolm X on the Afro-American problem as a world problem, with Dick Gregory and Abdulrahman Muhammad Babu.

December 16, 1964 Malcolm at "Harvard Law School Forum" (50 minutes). Malcolm X on the African Revolution and its impact on the American Negro.

December 31, 1964 Malcolm X delivers "Speech to Mississippi Youth, New York City" (15 minutes). Malcolm tells a group of young people, "think for yourself."

1964 Malcolm X's "Press Conference in New York City" (7 minutes). Malcolm X calls press conference to clarify position in the struggle, regarding politics and nonviolence.

INTERNET SOURCES

Carson, Clayborne. Editor. *Autobiography of Martin Luther King, Jr.* (among credible quotable sources, where Malcolm X and other black leaders are mentioned or discussed): http://www.stanford.edu/group/King/publications,autobiography/chp_21.htm.

Formwalt, Lee W. "Moving Forward by recalling the Past . . .": http://members.surfsouth.com/~mtzion/movementshistory.htm.

Gittinger, Ted. & Allen Fisher. "Lyndon B. Johnson Champions the Civil Rights Act of 1964." http://www.archives.gov/publications/prologue/2004/summer/civil-rights-act-1.html.

Pastors & Ministers. "Eulogy for the Young Victims of the Sixteenth Street Baptist Church Bombing" delivered at Sixth Avenue Baptist Church in Birmingham, Alabama: http://www.stanford.edu/group/King/speeches/pub/Eulogy_for_the_martyred_children.html.

President John F. Kennedy's "June 11, 1963, speech to American people": http://www.jfklibrary.org/j061163.htm.

President Lyndon B. Johnson's "American Promise Speech of March 15, 1965, to American People": http://www.lbjlib.utexas.edu/johnson/archives.hom/speeches.hom/650315.asp.

Ture, Kwame (Stokely Carmichael). "Speech on Black Power and the Black People of America." http://www.americanrhetoric.com/speeches/stokelycarmichaelblackpower.html.

MANUSCRIPT COLLECTIONS

Alex Haley Papers at Schomburg Center for Research in Black Culture. The New York Public Library.

Beinecke Rare Book Library, Yale University, New Haven, Connecticut.

Boston University Library's Special Collection (Martin Luther King, Jr., Papers).

C. Eric Lincoln Papers. Special Collections of Clark Atlanta University

Du Bois Centre and Archives, Accra, Ghana, West Africa.

Ghana National Archives, Accra, Ghana, West Africa (Kwame Nkrumah/Malcolm X/Graham Du Bois' Correspondence).

Mooreland-Spingarn Research Center of Howard University.

Morehouse College Special King Collections (Official Acquisition), Atlanta, Georgia.

Northeastern University Special Collections, Boston, Massachusetts.

The Malcolm X Project & Oral History Project at Columbia University, New York.

The Papers of Malcolm X at Schomburg Center for Research in Black Culture of New York Public Library, Harlem, New York.

INDEX

About the Authors

A.B. Assensoh, who holds a Ph.D. in History, is a professor emeritus of Indiana University and, currently, a courtesy professor in the History Department of University of Oregon. He is the author or co-author of several books and numerous refereed articles, including the co-authored *African Military History in History and Politics, 1900–Present* (2001) and *African Political History & Politics: Jomo Kenyatta, Kwame Nkrumah & Julius K. Nyerere* (1998). He has also held Fulbright-Hays Faculty fellowship in Southeast Asia as well as postdoctoral fellowships at Harvard University and University of Oxford in the United Kingdom. At Stanford University, he previously served as director of Research and associate editor of the Martin Luther King, Jr. Papers Project (now an institute).

Yvette M. Alex-Assensoh holds a Ph.D. in Political Science from the Ohio State University, and the Juris Doctorate (J.D.) degree from the Maurer School of Law of Indiana University. She moved from Indiana University as Dean of the Office for Women's Affairs (OWA) and professor of political science to University of Oregon to become vice president for Equity and Inclusion and professor of political science. She is the author or co-author of several books and refereed articles, including *African Military History and Politics, 1900–Present* (2001); co-author of *Newcomers, Outsiders and Insiders: Immigrants and American Racial Politics in the Early Twenty-First Century* (2010); and *Neighborhoods, Family, and Political Behavior in Urban America* (1998). Alex-Assensoh—a Fulbright Scholar in Croatia and ACE fellow—and A.B. Assensoh are parents of two sons, Kwadwo Stephen Alex Assensoh and Livingston Alex Kwabena Assensoh.